Christmas 1985

Shirley & Alex

with love from

Joyce

Travels of a Commentator

Dorian Williams

Travels of
a Commentator

Methuen · London

First published in Great Britain in 1985
by Methuen London Ltd
11 New Fetter Lane, London EC4P 4EE
Copyright © 1985 by Dorian Williams
Made and printed in Great Britain
by Richard Clay (The Chaucer Press) Ltd
Bungay, Suffolk

British Library Cataloguing in Publication Data

Williams, Dorian, *1914–1985*
    Travels of a Commentator.
    1. Sports journalism—Great Britain   2. Television
    broadcasting of sports—Great Britain   3. Horse
    sports—Great Britain
    I. title
    791.45'5   PN5124.S65

    ISBN 0–413–58210–8

for Fred Viner

with whom I had so much happiness
and friendship in our BBC days

Contents

Illustrations

Acknowledgement and thanks for permission to reproduce photographs are due to Ernst G. Wertheimer for plate 1b; United Press Photos for plates 2a, 3a, 3b and 5b; Keystone Press Agency for plate 2b; German National Tourist Office for plates 4b and 7b; Findlay Davidson for plates 6a, 6b, 7a, 10a and 13b; Leslie Lane for plates 8a, 8b, 10b, 12a, 12b and 13a; Syndication International for plates 11a and 11b; French Government Tourist Office for plates 14a and 14b; M. Ansell for plates 15a and 15b; Ib Nicolajsen for plate 16c.

Foreword

It always seems to me that when great sporting occasions from all over the world are reported on the air or in the press the general public is informed only about the salient facts: who won, who was disqualified, who failed, who fell – who had a 'positive' test. The more important the event the more so this is likely to be, as space is at such a premium, with some fifty sports jockeying for position on the sports pages or in the television schedules. Yet it was so often my experience – as, I am sure, it was of other commentators and reporters – that many of the most interesting incidents – amusing, unexpected, emotional – never get reported at all; there is just not the space or the time. But it is incidents such as those that may well prove to be the most unforgettable of all. As far as I am concerned personally, certainly they seem to have remained most vividly in my memory. Yet often I have to think quite hard to recall who won a certain medal at a particular Olympic Games.

When I embarked on my career as a television commentator over thirty years ago – quite by chance incidentally – obviously I looked forward to seeing medals won and lost, moments of high tension and drama, triumphs and disasters. But I am sure I never imagined that I would one day, for instance, find myself part of a human chain stopping horses from being swept away in a bubbling, raging torrent; or that I would spend the early hours of one bitterly cold morning in a completely empty Olympic stadium awaiting the arrival of a 'ghost' horse; or that I would ever be forced to lie prostrate on the ground for ten minutes while grim-faced Russians 'passed by on the other side'; or that I would receive a public rebuke from the Chairman of the Olympic Committee. Certainly I never envisaged myself escorting a BBC camera crew – jeans, anoraks, the lot – to a smart social function at one of Rome's most exclusive clubs, let alone enjoying a hilarious luncheon with the paralysed octogenarian Sultan of Jahore in his pink marble palace. At one Olympic Games I even found myself playing gooseberry to two of the most famous personalities in the equestrian world; at another I shared my commentary box with a prime minister; at a third – but I could go on indefinitely.

Hence this book. It is my genuine belief that many ordinary people find such 'behind-the-scenes' experiences, accounts of which never normally see the light of day, as of much interest as the bare statistical facts; even more so perhaps.

They have provided many memorable moments for me. I hope that they will for my readers.

Part I

Eight Olympiads 1948–1976

Chapter 1

First and Best

Stockholm 1956

I had been working for the BBC as their equestrian commentator for some four years, but in the spring of 1956 I was delighted to receive an official invitation to join their team for the Olympic Games in Stockholm in June. Officially the 1956 Games were held in Melbourne, but because of the quarantine regulations in Australia it was impossible to take horses there, with the result that there were separate equestrian Olympics at Stockholm, similar to the Winter Olympics at Cortina in the Italian Alps. What was particularly pleasing was the fact that as there were suddenly two vacancies in the British Horse Society's party of supporters, I was able to take Jennifer, whom I had married two months earlier. Obviously I preferred to be accommodated with her in the somewhat spartan hostel accommodation at the university rather than on my own in the fairly posh hotel where Peter Dimmock and the BBC team were staying. There were two other reasons why I was very pleased to be going to Stockholm. The first was that my father, Colonel V. D. S. Williams, who had trained the British three-day event team, had been appointed *chef de mission* of the whole British squad; the second was that my stepmother, Brenda, with Lorna Johnston, had been selected to represent Britain in the Grand Prix de Dressage, the first British riders ever to do so. Naturally she was thrilled to be riding in the Olympics, but had to survive quite an ordeal to do so.

Fearing that her horse, Pilgrim, on which she had won many hack classes before concentrating on dressage, might get over-excited in the Opening Ceremony, she asked if she could borrow another horse. Immediately the eventers offered her their spare horse: a smart, very sprightly grey six-year-old belonging to Kay Green, a great supporter of eventing. At this time very few people took dressage seriously, and those who did were considered by many people to take it too seriously. I remember a violent argument at a welcoming party shortly after we had arrived at Stockholm between Brenda and one of the British three-day event team, Bertie Hill, who stated bluntly that he thought that dressage was rubbish and need not be included in the three-day event at all. One cannot help feeling that the eventers and the show jumpers, who at that time believed even less in dressage than the eventers did, thought that it would be a joke to provide Brenda with a horse for the Opening Ceremony that they knew could be quite a handful – as it certainly was. It bucked and cavorted all the way round the arena, Brenda doing brilliantly to stay on; but when the British team took their salute in the centre of the arena her top hat was askew, her hunting tie was flying in the wind and she had lost both stirrups. It was all taken in good part, however, Brenda proving if nothing else that a dressage rider could manage a bucking bronco. In fact, before taking up dressage she had been brilliant across country in the hunting field. But it had been agony for her family to watch from the stands.

The Opening Ceremony was a magnificent spectacle. It was in the stadium which had been built for the 1912 Olympic Games, and was therefore of rather more aesthetic value than modern stadia, and took place in the presence of the King and Queen of Sweden, who arrived in an open carriage escorted by a squadron of the Royal Svea Life Guards, in their pale blue uniforms, on chestnut horses. There was dancing and singing and music from massed bands, and, of course, Swedish gymnastics; all very impressive, and as is usual on these occasions a little protracted, with lengthy speeches, for the most part in Swedish.

After the three-day event and dressage finished on the Tuesday afternoon we all went out to walk the cross-country course. We had to go in convoy as the whereabouts had been kept a close secret. It had been rumoured that the course was very big; indeed, there had been criticisms from various welfare and anti-cruelty to animals organisations. Certainly it appeared enormous to me, but the general consensus of opinion among the experts was that it was fair, and likely to sort out the men from the boys, as it was designed to. As we walked the course, the weather was ideal: bright with a cool breeze, but dark clouds were lowering beyond the hills. Sure enough, during the night we were woken by heavy rain falling on the wooden roof of the hostel; it continued as we dressed, breakfasted and boarded our coach. When we reached the course we found it to be very different from the previous afternoon. Parts of the course were boggy, parts – the tracks – were slippery and in places there was running water.

The first of the fifty-seven competitors, an Australian, started over the course at 8.00 a.m., it being about 9.00 a.m. when he reached the cross-country having, apparently, had a fall on the steeplechase course. With my producer Ronnie Noble – my commentary was to be dubbed on to the Swedish television film later – I followed the progress of the first few horses on the huge electric score-board at the top of the hill near the start and finish. As a horse reached a fence a light went up: white if clear, green for a refusal, red for a fall. The second rider was eliminated at Fence 22, a huge trakhener – the first hint of the trouble that this fence was to cause. The third rider, the first in the German team, went well until he reached the very last fence on the course, a big drop, at which he fell. The next, a Swiss, had four falls; a rider from Turkey was carried off in a helicopter after falling at the seventh; the first American rider suffered the same fate after falling at the last. Then to everyone's relief Capuzzo from Italy and Baklychine from Russia went clear, one after the other, the Finnish rider in between them having lost his way on the steeplechase course and been eliminated. But it was not a very encouraging start.

We decided that it was now time to take to our Land Rover and see some of the performances at close quarters. The rain had ceased, but it was still very over-cast. To our delight we saw both our own Laurence Rook, the first to go for Britain, on Ted Marsh's magnificent bright bay Dublin Show Champion, Wild Venture, and Mullers from Ireland gallop past going really well; in contrast to a Frenchman who had a refusal and a fall at Fence 22, the trakhener, while a Portuguese rider reached us having had no less than five falls and a refusal.

We waited anxiously for the next from the British team,
Countryman III, ridden by Bertie Hill who had originally
owned the horse but from whom my father had bought it for
the Queen, or rather so that it could run in the Queen's name.
Countryman was, in fact, owned jointly by the Queen, the
Queen Mother, the Duke of Beaufort and my father. Wanting
to follow his progress round the whole course, and at the same
time see him tackle the now crucial trakhener at Fence 22 –
there had been no less than eight falls, refusals or eliminations
at this fence by the time that Bertie Hill and Countryman
arrived – we found a vantage point where, using our glasses,
we could see both the score-board and Fence 22.

The lights on the score-board seemed to be going up
quicker than for any other rider as this great combination
scorched round the course: 16 and 17 clear, 18 clear, the long
gallop to complex 19, 20, 21 clear. Down below us we could
see them approaching Fence 22. It seemed as though
Countryman had already taken off, on the right-hand side of
the fence; then we realised with horror that actually he had
stopped. In fact, as he took off the bank had given way;
Countryman had slipped down into the stream at the bottom,
but having attempted to take off, his front legs were already
over the heavy larch pole. Hoping that somehow the horse
would struggle over, Bertie remained on top, sliding off only
when it was obvious that the horse was stuck – sixty penalties
for a fall. With the soldier on duty at the fence he attempted
desperately to push him over. No good! Then suddenly we
saw a figure running down the hill from near Fence 23. It was
Colonel Gordon Cox-Cox, Director of the Badminton Horse
Trials. With his great experience he knew that when a horse is
stuck on a fence it is much easier, because of weight distribu-
tion, to push it backwards, rather than to pull it forwards.
Bertie at once accepted this from Cox-Cox, but others started
to argue. If he went backwards it would be another twenty
faults for a refusal; if he were pushed and pulled over the fence,
then he would be penalised only the sixty penalties for a fall.
But the authority of Gordon Cox-Cox prevailed and within a
few seconds – though it seemed like minutes – Countryman
was safely back at the top of the bank.

Hurtling down the hill in our Land Rover, ostensibly to

help, we arrived just in time to see Bertie remounted and, incredibly, calmly setting sail again at this formidable trakhener. He popped over it as if there had never been any trouble at all, and galloped on; a performance of remarkable courage. We hurried on to our next vantage point at Fence 38, a huge log pile across a clearing in a wood, but looking back as we drove away I could see the stewards cordoning off the right-hand side of the fence. If only they had done it before the arrival of Countryman! We could see also the green and red lights against Fence 22 on the giant electric score-board. Arriving in our Land Rover at Fence 38 I saw the Queen, standing close to the fence, stop-watch in hand, with the Duke of Beaufort, Colonel John Miller and others. Seeing me, the Duke of Beaufort beckoned me across.

'Any news?' he asked.

I described quickly what had happened at Fence 22. At this moment one could hear in the distance the stewards' whistles warning of an approaching horse.

'You cannot possibly be right', said the Queen. 'Here's Countryman coming now, he's the next horse,' – she tapped her stop-watch – 'and he's reached us in a quicker time than any other horse so far.'

'I can assure you, ma'am', I started, but she turned away as Countryman approached up the path through the trees. He was there and gone in a flash, flying the massive logs almost with disdain and disappearing down the slope through the trees.

'He certainly had a lot of mud on him', the Duke conceded.

'We'll see', said the Queen, boarding her Land Rover while we returned to ours. We drove quickly to the end of the course where the score-board confirmed the facts: No. 48, Countryman III, a green and a red light at Fence 22, but the rest white. Eighty faults. It could so easily have been clear. In fact, had it not been for those eighty faults, Countryman would have won the silver medal, just four points behind August Lutke Westhues, the individual winner from Germany; but had there not been loss of time in addition while the horse was extricated from the trakhener he could even have won the gold for the Queen. As a matter of interest, after the right-hand side of the fence had been cordoned off out of the

remaining twenty-two starters, there were only two falls and
two refusals.

Nevertheless it was with great relief that we saw the white
light go up at Fence 22 when Frank Weldon, last of the British
team, went round on Kilbarry, despite what I can only refer to
as an optical illusion. I was watching the score-board with my
father and Diana Weldon, Frank's wife. I had always been a
little nervous of Diana, ever since she told me off for referring
to Kilbarry's excellent temperament; apparently he was
extremely highly strung and presented Frank with a real
problem in the dressage arena. Now, as we all anxiously
watched the score-board, I was to realise how human she was.
Kilbarry had had a refusal at Fence 7, a fairly innocuous post
and rails which he had approached at too oblique an angle.
After that it was all plain sailing: clear 15, clear the two
complexes, clear 21. Now for 22, but nothing happened. We
waited for what seemed like minutes: no light at 22. Then
suddenly the white light was on at 24. Looking back we all saw
that it was on at 22; also 23. How had we missed it? Perhaps we
were over-anxious, perhaps the lights had been late coming
on, but it had been a nerve-racking two or three minutes.
Diana's relief, as Frank's wife, and my father's relief as team
trainer, were understandable; but mine was no less intense,
perhaps from a sense of patriotism, for that built-in computer
within us which always seems to be able to work these things
out before one can work them out factually had already
convinced us that as long as Frank got safely round we should
go into the final phase, the show jumping, with a virtually
unbeatable lead over the Germans.

In the event we could afford twelve fences down at the start
of the last day and still win, which we did convincingly, in a
packed stadium, finishing with a score of 355.48 penalty
points over Germany's 475.91, with Canada third, another
100 points behind. The lap of honour by our three-day
eventers will be an abiding memory as long as I live. The three
great bay horses – Countryman, in fact, was bay/brown –
made a marvellously impressive picture as they galloped
round the arena, Frank Weldon in uniform, the other two in
scarlet. Not for the last time in my career as a commentator did
I find myself so choked with emotion that for a few moments I

was unable to speak. Frank Weldon also won the individual bronze, with Laurence Rook in sixth place and Bertie Hill twelfth, but had it not been for Fence 22 –!

Nevertheless we had plenty to celebrate, and we certainly did: on the Royal Yacht Britannia, at the invitation of the Queen. About forty of us had been invited. The water was a little choppy and a fairly strong wind was blowing which distressed the ladies who had spent pounds having their hair done; no hats had been the instruction for the ladies, but gloves? – no one seemed to know. When we reached the top of the heaving gang-plank the Queen was there to greet us with Prince Philip; she looked immaculate, in a dark blue dress and wearing that wonderful cluster brooch with her usual lovely string of pearls, he was in a lounge suit. When Jennifer and I reached the head of the queue the Queen laughed as she shook my hand. 'You were quite right', she said, and for several moments we talked about the dramas of the morning. Never a moment did she give any sign of disappointment at Countryman's unfortunate fall which had denied her the individual gold medal, let alone bitterness; she seemed to accept it in just the same way as less than three months earlier, her mother had accepted the extraordinary collapse of Devon Loch fifty yards from the winning post when winning the Grand National. Truly our royal family have an enviable sense of sportsmanship, which could well be emulated by others.

In fact, the Queen was in tremendous form that evening, mixing with all her guests, obviously enjoying herself, being with people who were as devoted to horses and equestrian sport as she was. We were allowed to wander more or less at random over the yacht, which was very much larger than I had expected and, for a landlubber, fascinating. Catching us peering into the ward room laid up for dinner for about twenty, one of the equerries kindly took us in and showed us some of the wonderful silver, the cleverly practical furniture and the pictures. Subtly, but quite firmly, we were left in no doubt as to when we were expected to depart which we did contentedly, feeling that we had been privileged to share with the Queen herself the celebration of Britain's victory.

The Grand Prix de Dressage started early next morning. Brenda, my stepmother, was the fourth to go, so she had been up since dawn. Perhaps she had been 'working in' too long; perhaps it was a case of nerves, Brenda being the first British rider ever to compete in Olympic dressage. Certainly Pilgrim's performance was disappointing. After entering at a kind of four-time canter he never really settled and finished with a score of 616, compared with that of the Swedish St Cyr, the ultimate winner, of 860; even Lorna Johnstone, the second British rider, with Rosie's Dream, had a score of 655, finishing twenty-first, four places ahead of Brenda. Inevitably there was a certain disappointment in the Williams camp, but it was not allowed to cloud the success of my father's three-day event team and the brilliant performance by his find, Countryman III.

It was the first time that I had watched Grand Prix Dressage. I have to admit that the first two sessions – the first twenty-two horses with an hour's break in the middle – was quite enough. It was not only that I found it repetitive – I appreciated top-class equitation even less then than I do now – but I became very disenchanted with the judging. The German judge had German competitors in the first three places; the Swedish judge had all the Swedish horses at the top; the Danish judge gave the remarkable Danish rider, Liz Hartel, twelve marks higher than anybody else. The other two judges, a Chilean and Belgian, might have been judging different competitions: their scores were often as much as forty or fifty marks apart. Sadly, one still sees these wide variations in top-level dressage judging, which cannot do much to popularise the sport; not unnaturally people become sceptical. We were sad to miss Liz Hartel's test in the afternoon as with immense courage she had overcome polio to win a silver medal at Helsinki in 1952, an achievement repeated at Stockholm. Fortunately, however, she came twice to the Horse of the Year Show to give exhibitions on her Olympic horse, Jubilee.

It so happened that at the same time that the equestrian Olympics were being held in Stockholm there was a semi-final round of the Davis Cup in which Britain was playing Sweden. Jennifer being very keen on tennis, we decided, not too reluctantly – we were not televising it – to forego the rest of the dressage and make our way out to the tennis on the outskirts of Stockholm. We had no option but to go by underground and although everyone told us how simple it was we frequently found ourselves on wrong trains and eventually took two hours to reach the tennis. To our relief, knowing that they had a hired car, we found that we were sitting immediately behind two British supporters: Colonel 'Babe' Moseley and Kay Green.

'Babe' had been a leading National Hunt amateur rider, but now he weighed eighteen stone and was very stout. A great character, with an uncharacteristically high-pitched voice, he was a dedicated supporter of eventing, invariably travelling with the team as assistant manager. He was a bachelor. Kay had come to England as a tiny Belgian refugee in the First World War, had been adopted by the Recketts (Blue) family and inherited much of their wealth. She married, first, Henry Green, who played the drums in the orchestra at Harrow when I was there, and later became the first head of racecourse security. They were divorced, but their son showed promise as an eventer, his horse being selected as reserve for Stockholm – the horse that Brenda rode at the Opening Ceremony.

During the afternoon I leaned forward and asked Babe if they would give us a lift back to the centre of Stockholm. Much to my surprise he said that it really would not be very convenient, but gave no further explanation. They left early, but we stayed until the last match was finished before attempting to find our way home by underground. The journey, even more difficult than the earlier journey, took us so long that we decided to miss the reception that was being given at the Swedish Embassy that night. We were having supper in the hostel when everyone returned from the reception.

'Have you heard the news?' we were immediately asked. 'No – what?' 'Babe and Kay have just announced their engagement.' No wonder they did not want us to accompany them back from the tennis. Indeed, they must have been none too pleased to see us arrive at the tennis, imagining that there they were bound to be undisturbed. At a reception next day at the Royal Palace, in the magnificent Royal State Hall used for the opening of Parliament, built in 1730, they apologised profusely. I was to find myself playing gooseberry, at a future Olympics, to an even better known couple.

The show jumping – team and individual were run together

– took place on the final Sunday, immediately before the
Closing Ceremony. It was the first time that an Olympic event
had been held on a Sunday and it caused many raised eyebrows, particularly, oddly enough, among the British. It was
rumoured that the Queen would not attend, and there was
speculation, too, when the royal party including, of course,
the Queen, left before the end; but with the show jumping
running two hours late this was not altogether surprising as
obviously they had to keep to their flight schedule – or it may
have been the Royal Yacht catching the tide.

The event was certainly a marathon, due firstly to each
horse being given a starting time, which had to be adhered to,
even if the previous horse had been eliminated. Secondly, and
worse, there was a combination of fences which caused almost
universal havoc. The fifth fence was a double consisting of
parallels, the first part being birch poles with a spread of 5 ft
7 in, the second, 28 ft away – an awkward distance – a pair of
gates with another spread 5 ft 7 in. About six strides further
on was a set of twelve tightly packed poles – no less – over 7 ft
of water. In all, these three fences comprised twenty-six poles.
The preceding fence, rather like an upturned trough, described as a South African pigsty, tended to surprise the horses
which, having lost their impulsion, then crashed into either
the double or the upright over the water, or probably both. In
the first round alone I calculated that the rebuilding of these
two fences took over an hour. During my commentary I
referred to the double as a box of Swedish matches. Other
commentators heard this, the name becoming generally
accepted, even finding its way into newspaper reports, which,
I was told later, did not amuse the course builder, Greve
Lewenhaupt. Before long this complex of fences became
something of a farce, which was unfortunate, as the course
was otherwise a real Olympic course, as is shown by the fact
that only one from the first horses of each team had 8 faults or
less; only two from the second horses of each team had 8 faults
or less; and only four of the third horses, the best, had 8 faults
or less. It was more or less the same in the second round, with
only Hans Winkler, from Germany, having a clear round,
which was all the more remarkable in that in the first round,
while jumping the last but one fence, described as Garden

Fence from the Riviera, a 5 ft 3 in upright, he had come down on the pommel of the saddle, giving himself a most painful injury. It was rumoured that he would not be able to jump in the second round, ruining Germany's chances of both the team and individual gold medal. But he did, though in great agony, which was quite obvious to the spectators.

'How are you going to explain that in your commentary?' asked my producer, Ronnie Noble. A problem indeed; similar to one with which Brian Johnston recently found himself faced when an English batsman was hit on the 'box', as it is euphemistically termed.

Supported by Alfons Lutke-Westhues, whose brother August had already won a silver medal in the three-day event, riding Ala and Fritz Thiedemann on Meteor, Germany inevitably won the gold, a superb performance in that it was Germany's first participation in the Games since 1936. Halla, Ala and Meteor were all three Puissance-type horses, the kind that are needed to win gold medals, of which there are only a very limited number in the world. Italy had two such horses, Merano and Uruguay, ridden by the d'Inzeo brothers. Their third horse Pagora, which had over 20 faults in each round, was a good but not a great horse. It was enough, however, to give them the silver with 66 faults, behind Germany's 40. Britain, with only one great or Puissance-type horse, Wilf White's Nizefela, and two good horses, Peter Robeson's Scorchin and Pat Smythe's Flanagan, did wonderfully to be only three points behind Italy for the bronze. Ironically it was Nizefela's famous and much loved kick-back that earned Britain the vital 4 faults that cost us the silver. Landing clear over the seventh fence, which was a wall with parallel poles behind it, 4 ft high and 6 ft 8 in wide, he kicked back, dislodging the top pole. But for this mistake he would also have won the individual silver. At Helsinki, in 1952, the unfortunate Wilf White and Nizefela, so often referred to as the full back of the British team, had lost the individual gold as a result of a dubious decision at the water. Now at Stockholm they were unlucky once again. Wilf's comment afterwards was, simply, 'Well, that's how it is isn't it? There was nothing wrong with the horse.' Pat Smythe, who was the first lady ever to ride in the Olympic show jumping, had the greatest

ovation of all on entering the stadium. No one could possibly
pretend that Britain was in any way disgraced, yet surprisingly on our returning home so many seemed disappointed
that we had not won everything. This, probably, was because
in seven Nations Cup (Team Events) in 1956 Britain had only
once been beaten, by Italy at Ostend: but an Olympic course is
very different to a Nations Cup course and it demands
Puissance-type horses. Had Foxhunter been available it might
have been different: but he was then nearing the end of his
great career, in which he had won seventy-eight international
competitions: in fact, he was to retire six weeks after the
Stockholm Olympics, having achieved his final win at
Dublin.

Apart from the eliminations, of which there were twenty-
four, the worst score at Stockholm was 56¼ for the Brazilian
Oliviera de Meneses; he scored most of his faults at the box of
matches. Many others had scores of between forty and fifty.
Amongst those eliminated were two riders from Cambodia.
At the Opening Ceremony there was some surprise that while
their flag and their placard were carried, there were no competitors. When they arrived two days later and were asked
why they had missed the Opening they replied that they had
not realised that Sweden was so far!

In addition to those already mentioned many of the most
famous show jumpers, pre-War and post-War, took part,
including Francisco Goyago and Carlos Figueroa from Spain,
both winners of the King George V Cup at Britain's Royal
International; Carlos Delia and Pedro Mayorga from Argentina; Pierre Jonquères d'Oriola and Bernard de Fombelle from
France; Nelson Pessoa from Brazil; Billy Ringrose and Kevin
Barry from Ireland; Bill Steinkraus, Frank Chapot and Hugh
Wiley from America; and from Sweden Anders Gernandt
who was to become Sweden's immensely popular equestrian
commentator, and a great personal friend of mine. What a
thrill it was for a young (youngish!) commentator to meet all
these famous riders, many of whom became close acquain-
tances if not personal friends!

The Closing Ceremony was due to start at 6.00 p.m., and
our plane was supposed to leave three hours later. In fact the
competition did not finish until 8.00 p.m. Fortunately our

charter plane, an ancient Dakota, agreed to a delay, but, sadly, we were only able to watch the start of the Closing Ceremony. I doubt that it bore very much resemblance to that in Los Angeles twenty-eight years later! We finally left at 10.30 p.m., trundling through the night, eventually to arrive at Northolt in the early hours.

The Stockholm Olympics are still the Games that I look back to with most affection; perhaps because like the Winter Olympics they were confined to one sport. Certainly on many occasions since 1956 I have regretted that the authorities did not gradually 'separate' the Olympics, replacing the Olympic Games with an Olympic Year, the different sports taking place all over the world; thus, inevitably, reducing all the nationalism and politicising which is nothing to do with the Olympic movement and, indeed, has gone a long way towards ruining it. Stockholm, 1956, was such a very happy occasion, enjoyed by everyone at whatever level they were involved: organiser, competitor, spectator – or commentator.

London 1948

Stockholm was not, in fact, my first Olympics. I had, unexpectedly, been very much involved in the 1948 Olympics in London. Almost at the last minute my father, who was on the organising committee, asked me to do the public-address commentary on the dressage and show-jumping phases of the three-day event held at Aldershot – there was no public address at all for the cross-country. The previous year I had become the official 'announcer', as it was then called, at the International Horse Show at the White City. I accepted happily, but was disconcerted to find that announcements had to be made in French as well as in English. As a precaution I took with me a young doctor, Neil Saunders, who was also a talented composer and spoke French fluently. We had enormous fun attempting to translate technical terms into French, our efforts frequently producing roars of laughter from the audience; which was probably quite a relief as according to my diary the dressage was 'long and very boring'.

The show-jumping competition at Wembley took place on 14 August, individual and team events being run concurrently. When at Aldershot a few days earlier Mike Ansell, who

by now was the show-jumping supremo in Britain, had asked
me to do the public address, I was delighted to accept, even
mentioning in my diary the 'wonderful privilege of being the
announcer and commentator at the Olympic Games'. I felt,
too, that as only names, numbers and faults were involved I
could manage the announcements in French as well as in
English. I had been given to understand that if, as was quite
possible, the show jumping overran, then the last part of it
would be televised, the television being all set up for the
Closing Ceremony. The BBC would then take my public-
address commentary, in both English and French, rather like
the Eurovision Song Contest. Mike Ansell, never one to miss
an opportunity, had asked Jack Webber, the Secretary General
of the British Show Jumping Association, to compile a few
notes on the history of the sport which I was to read out – in
English only – should the jumping be televised. Conscientious
as ever, Jack Webber produced three foolscap pages. As soon
as I heard that the jumping was being televised I started
reading this lengthy spiel. Although the next horse to jump
was in the ring, waiting, I carried on, as not having previously
read the script I had no idea where I could conveniently stop,
but I knew that there was a splendid peroration designed to
impress the largely lay public which had really come to
Wembley for the Closing Ceremony: a captive audience if
ever there was one. After several minutes I noticed someone
walking across from the stands to our commentary position,
more or less in the centre of the arena which I shared with the
judges – and Mike Ansell. It was Lord Burghley, later the
Marquess of Exeter, Chairman of the Olympic Games
Organising Committee. Courteously, but with the natural
authority of an aristocrat, he asked me to stop talking and
allow the event which was already running very late to
continue: we wanted to speed it up, not delay it. 'Please
announce the next horse, at once.' I felt very humiliated, and
frustrated in that I could not explain that I was only doing
what I had been told. It hurt all the more because David
Burghley, an Olympic gold medallist himself in the 120 yards
hurdles in 1924, had been my hero since my schooldays, when
hurdling had been my principal athletic achievement. Later he
was to become a great friend, and was kind enough to write

the foreword for my book, *Pendley and a Pack of Hounds*. This, however, was not the end of my somewhat ignominious introduction to the Olympics. Knowing that the event was being televised I felt obliged to make a few comments, in English, about the riders and horses as they went round the course. I tried to keep my remarks to a minimum, but felt that just to announce each horse and rider, in two languages, then give their faults when they finished, in two languages, would not exactly create much excitement – or interest amongst the television viewers seeing show jumping for the first time.

This time it was the secretary to the Jury of Appeal who was to be seen striding across to our commentary position. By the time he had reached us, dodging a horse or two on its way in or out, he had worked himself into quite a state. On no account must I speak once a horse had started its round. The rules were quite clear; it had to be exactly the same for every horse in the competition and I had only started speaking during the jumping in the last few minutes (when we were on television). Furthermore, it was distracting; in any case anything that I said should be in two languages. I had to admit to myself that there had been a certain amount of sh-shing when I spoke. I had no option but to limit myself to introducing the rider when he came in and giving his faults when he went out. I felt quite deflated and my initial enthusiasm at being officially part of the Olympic Games was quickly evaporating. But when Colonel Harry Llewellyn came in on his seven-year-old Foxhunter, after 3 previous riders had been eliminated, and completed the course with only 16 faults my spirits rose considerably; in fact, in the whole competition only 6 horses had less than 16, while 19 out of 44 were eliminated. Britain now seemed certain to win a team medal, as they did, the bronze; Foxhunter finished equal seventh with Kilgeddin, also owned by Harry Llewellyn and ridden by Colonel Henry Nichol, the third member of the team, and Colonel Arthur Carr on Monty finished nineteenth. Mexico won the gold and Spain the silver.

There was, too, a little light relief, which could not fail to relax me however tense the competition and the commentator. Again and again horses faulted at the two water jumps. With increasing regularity poles or, not infrequently, riders

splashed in, each time displacing water, which because of the
drought that summer was in very short supply, and was
apparently especially scarce at Wembley. Came the moment
when the Clerk of the Course was instructed to fill up the
ditches, but no water came out of the hoses. It was checked
that there was nothing wrong with the taps or valves so a
frantic message was sent to the chief engineer, but he, it
seemed, was powerless to help; the London Water Board had
cut off the supply at midday and as it was a Saturday there was
no one on duty. The water ditches had to become dry ditches,
which together with an almost waterless water jump cannot
have made it any easier for the later competitors who kept up a
steady flow of complaints; but their complaints were effectively silenced when the very last competitor, General Mariles
Cortes from Mexico, had just 4 faults – and those were
deliberate. Knowing that he could win if he had less than 8
faults he decided to ignore the water, merely popping over the
fence, having seen the majority of competitors getting up so
much speed to clear the water – increasingly unlikely with
horses seeing the last 4 ft of the 16 ft 'water jump' dry ground
– that they were then unable to steady in time to jump a 5 ft
3 in red wall a few strides away. In fact General Cortes had
taken a considerable risk as, going slowly to guarantee his
accuracy over the fences, he incurred 2¼ time penalties; but he
still won the gold medal. Twenty years later I was, indirectly,
to have a rather sad association with him.

The jumping did not finish until 6.00 p.m., which was
supposed to be the time at which the whole Closing
Ceremony was to end. But at 6.00 p.m. I was, in fact,
supposed to be at a little village called Marsworth, near Tring
in Hertfordshire, two miles from Pendley Manor, my family
home, which at the end of the war I had turned into a Centre of
Adult Education. The drama group which we had formed a
year earlier had been invited to perform at the local fête some
scenes from Shakespeare presented at Pendley the previous
week. It had been intended that they should be the climax of
the fête, but owing to my sudden involvement with the
Olympic Games it was agreed that they would be performed
at 7.00 p.m. instead of 6.00 p.m.

As soon as the presentations were over I made a dash for my

car, disappointed as I was to miss the Closing Ceremony though, in fact, I had no official seat from which to watch it, as the commentary box had been hastily dismantled. Actually being involved personally in the Games, I felt that it seemed a pity to miss the closing pageantry, especially the massed choirs singing the Olympic hymn to the tune of the 'Londonderry Air' with words specially written by A. P. Herbert, the second verse of which went:

> If all the lands could run with all the others
> And work as sweetly as the young men play
> Lose with a laugh, and battle but as brothers
> Loving to win – but not in every way.

A fine sentiment which certainly would not be out of place today.

But the fête had to take priority – inconceivable today, surely! – and by the time the stadium was ringing to A. P. Herbert's words I was in Marsworth, which I had somehow managed to reach in fifty minutes. My arrival was the sign for an immediate start to the scenes from Shakespeare. While the first episode – the witches from *Macbeth* – was being performed I hurriedly changed into my costume as Richard III for the coffin scene with Lady Anne, widow of Edward, Prince of Wales, played by the lovely Polly Elwes, later to marry Peter Dimmock. The setting for these scenes was a rather uneven clearing in some trees. The backcloth was a small marquee which was being used for the most popular side-show of the fête – live television. I had just delivered my opening lines –

> Villains! set down the corse, or by St Paul
> I'll make a corse of him that disobeys

– when to my horror through the canvas of the marquee I heard an all-too-familiar voice announcing 'the next to jump will be Commandant Garcia Cruz from Spain on Bizarro. Le prochain Cavalier est Commandant Garcia Cruz d'Espagne avec Bizarro. Captain Kasar from Turkey was eliminated. Le Captain Kasar de Turquie est eliminé.' The show jumping from Wembley which had been recorded was now being

transmitted, and was being featured in the television side-
show in the marquee. Polly, not surprisingly, became giggly
and when just as my voice started to announce another horse
the other side of the canvas she had to say 'Foul devil, for
God's sake hence and trouble us not' we both collapsed in
helpless laughter; as did the whole audience.

For a little longer we carried on, someone having turned
down the sound, but the worse was to come. We were just
reaching the climax when, dramatically, Richard declaims:

> I never sued to friend nor enemy:
> My tongue could never learn sweet soothing words

when suddenly from the loudspeakers above us there boomed
out words that were anything but soothing: 'The last bus for
Tring is leaving in five minutes', and the entire audience – all
twenty of them – rose and departed! (With strict petrol
rationing most people were dependent on public transport in
1948.) And so I was denied my splendid climax:

> This hand which for thy love did kill thy love
> Shall, for thy love, kill a far truer love.

My performance had been killed already. Twice in an
afternoon I had been cheated of my big chance, but under very
different circumstances; at the magnificent final day of the
fourteenth Olympiad and at a very small village fête. The
sublime and the ridiculous? Perhaps. Yet odd similarities were
to stem from these so different experiences. The week after the
Olympic Games I received, to my astonishment, a letter from
an important executive of the BBC with the name of
Lotbinière, thanking me for my splendid contribution to the
Olympic Games and informing me that I would shortly
receive a cheque; which I did, for £15. But not for a moment
then did I imagine that my somewhat inauspicious debut on
television would be the prelude to thirty years as the BBC's
equestrian commentator.

Oddly enough the little scenes from Shakespeare, performed first at Pendley and then at a few villages locally, were
so successful that the following year, 1949, we decided to

mount a full-scale performance of Shakespeare's *Henry VIII*. It went extremely well but, again, never for a moment did I imagine that it would build up into the annual Pendley Shakespeare Festival which now attracts audiences of over 15,000.

From little acorns – !

Chapter 2

Roman Holiday

Rome 1960

All the equestrian events were fitted into the second week of the Rome Olympics, which made it a very hectic week. But for me it had been hectic even before I arrived in Rome. The previous Saturday saw the end of the annual Pendley Shakespeare Festival, with the by then traditional midnight matinée. On the last night of the Festival both plays are performed, the first starting at 7.00 p.m., the second at 10.00 p.m. The plays in 1960 were *The Taming of the Shrew* and *Richard II*. As both were fairly lengthy productions, each attracting large audiences which had to be changed over at the end of the first play. It was 3.00 a.m. before I finally retired. I had, incidentally, been cubhunting that morning at High Havens, one of the most famous coverts in the Whaddon Chase country, which had meant my rising at 5.30 a.m. A lie-in was out of the question as I had to be at the airport mid-morning to meet up with a large group of British supporters, my BBC colleagues already being in Rome.

At the airport, we were still waiting to be called a full hour beyond the official departure time of our flight when an announcement was made to the effect that our plane would be delayed for at least two hours, having been late leaving Rome. At about 2.00 p.m. a further two-hour delay was announced. One of the party of supporters was Bob Hanson, father of the present Lord Hanson, a great patron of show jumping and the owner of such horses as Flanagan, Merely-a-Monarch and O'Malley. He was very much associated with transport having originally been involved with his family's famous Hanson Horse Transport in Yorkshire. His was not the sort of temperament to suffer delays easily. In fact, he was charging

all over the airport like an enraged bull. Suddenly he shouted
across the lounge, 'Follow me'. At first, as I did not then know
him particularly well, it did not occur to me that it was I whom
he was summoning. But then he called me by name.

'I've told them to put us on an Alitalia flight', he said. 'I saw
one waiting at the top of the runway.' Apparently at first he
was told that it was only in transit and could not take on new
passengers. But Bob did not brook any what he would regard
as irrelevant argument with the result that before many
minutes we were being whisked out to the Alitalia plane in an
airport car – a little to my embarrassment – leaving all our
fellow supporters stranded in the departure lounge. By this
time it did not surprise me that on boarding the plane we were
immediately ushered into the first-class compartment, nor
that despite the fact that it was after 3.00 p.m., as soon as the
plane had taken off we were regaled with a first-class lunch,
washed down with champagne.

After an incident-free flight we landed at Rome, but the
wrong side of the Capuchino airport. In those days Alitalia
used one side of Capuchino while all other airlines used the
other. Naturally, Bob Hanson's Rolls, which had been sent on
in advance with his faithful chauffeur Edward, was the wrong
side. It was Bob's intention to phone a message across, but
while waiting for a free callbox we were approached by the
mother of a friend of mine who recognised me and asked if we
were in trouble. I explained the situation, at which she
immediately offered to drive us into Rome. By a coincidence
the person she had come to meet was someone connected with
the oil industry whom Bob, also having interests in oil, knew
well. Realising that it would take a long time for Edward to
get the Rolls round to the other side of the airport, Bob
decided to accept the kind offer, arranging for an airport
official to phone the patient Edward, telling him to return to
Rome. When we reached my friend's car, however, it turned
out to be a mini. Bob Hanson was not only 6 ft 4 in, he was
also a big man in every way. The friend in oil was short, but
square. Fortunately at that time I was slim. Somehow we all
managed to squeeze into the mini, our luggage piled on top of
us. Bob was staying at the magnificent Excelsior Hotel on the
Via Veneto. I was being accommodated at a motel, that had

been commandeered by the BBC. On the way to the Excelsior my friend told us that two of her family were supposed to
be flying out on our original plane and were then meeting her
at the Opera. But with the plane so late it was obviously going
to be impossible for them to get to the Opera in time; she
therefore very kindly offered us their tickets. As it was a
performance of Tosca with Maria Callas singing how could
one refuse? For me this was indeed an unexpected bonus, as
unexpected as my first-class flight with the VIP treatment. A
good start, I thought, forgetting my tiredness.

The original plan was to drop Bob at the Excelsior, take me
to my motel, then go back to the Excelsior for sandwiches and
champagne before going on to the Opera. Unfortunately, in
the rush hour – and with the Olympic traffic – we did not
arrive at the Excelsior until it was obviously too late to go to
my motel, so we just had our smoked salmon sandwiches and
set off for a quite unforgettable evening at the Opera, arriving
back at the Excelsior at about midnight, when Bob insisted on
us having more smoked salmon sandwiches and champagne.
At about 1.00 a.m. Bob called a porter and told him to get me
a taxi. When after half an hour the porter had not re-appeared
Bob sent another to discover what had happened. Apparently
no taxi was obtainable, which was worrying as I was sure that
it was too far to walk to my hotel. Eventually, to my relief,
one turned up and, climbing in, I showed the address of my
motel to the driver: Hotel Pacifico, Via Medaglie D'Oro. As
the driver had not sounded too confident it did not surprise me
when, having made our way through the still heavy traffic and
found the Via Medaglie D'Oro, it became apparent that he had
no idea whatever of the whereabouts of my hotel. Twice we
drove up and down the street, then, pulling up at a petrol
station, with a gesture of despair, he summarily set me down.

Not a very promising situation; stranded in the middle of a
city that I did not know at three o'clock in the morning, with a
very heavy suitcase. Fortunately – and surprisingly – the
petrol station was still open. Sitting in the kiosk there was a
large, greasy man in a sweatshirt to whom I showed the
motel's address. Without speaking he just jerked his thumb
over his shoulder pointing behind him. To my astonishment I
saw that behind the garage was a narrow hotel entrance. Sure

enough the Pacifico. To my delight and relief, as I entered, I ran straight into Harold Abrahams, an old friend whose wife, Sybil Evers, for many years a leading member of the D'Oyly Carte Company, had actually been taking part in the Pendley Shakespeare Festival that had finished the previous night. Harold was in Rome both for BBC Radio and for the *Sunday Times*. Having been typing a report in the little coffee-shop that was also the hotel's restaurant, virtually taking up the whole ground floor, he had just come out for a breath of fresh air.

There was no one at the desk, but I knew my room number, eighty-four, so took the key off the hook, dutifully signing my name in the book. I wasted little time in staggering up to my landing and falling into the unused bed, one of two, in a room that seemed barely large enough for a single. I was quite unaware with whom I was sharing the room; a male, I assumed, though I was almost too tired to care. When I awoke comparatively early next morning – or more accurately later the same morning – my instructions being to present myself at the Press Centre at the Foro Italico by 9.00 a.m. for my accreditation card, my companion was still sleeping soundly, completely covered by a sheet. I tiptoed out of the room trying not to disturb him as he must have come in even later than I had. Over a cup of coffee I met my producer, Ronnie Noble.

The BBC was to record some of the Grand Prix de Dressage which was fortunate as once again, Brenda, my stepmother, was performing, but this time with Little Model on which for the last two years she had been the outstanding British competitor. As Little Model was, allegedly, a bad traveller Brenda, who could be somewhat paranoic about her horses, and my father had driven the whole way from England, taking Little Model out of the box in the early hours each morning and riding him for two or three hours along the verges. After an hour or two in the box he would be taken out again for another two or three hours. The journey lasted a fortnight, but it very much caught the imagination of the general public, taking up inches of space in the national press, though Brenda was not too pleased at being referred to as Galloping Grandma!

It was somewhat frustrating in Rome that no dressage

scores were announced until after the end of the whole event.
On Monday evening they announced only the names of the
five who were to take part in the reprise – Grand Prix Special,
as it would be called today. But why only five? Usually it was
twelve. In those days, apparently, it used to be left to the
discretion of the organisers; perhaps with no Italians in the
running they thought that five were enough. The general
opinion seemed to be – and not only amongst the British – that
had twelve gone forward to the reprise Brenda and Little
Model might very well have been included. That they had
done their best test ever all agreed; but there it was. The five
selected were Filatov and Kalita from Russia, St Cyr from
Sweden – winner in Stockholm four years earlier – Fischer
from Switzerland – though everyone thought it should have
been Chammartin who had been third in Helsinki and second
in Stockholm; and Neckermann from Germany whose test I
personally found very stodgy, if accurate; as I did eight years
later in Mexico. I was very surprised that the marks awarded
to the competitors on the first day were added to those in the
reprise, as this was not the usual practice. I was even more
surprised to discover that the result was not to be announced
until two full days later – after the judges had seen a film! Once
again I found it difficult not to be a little cynical about dressage
judging. To the delight of most of the British supporters the
beautifully fluent Russian Filatov won from Fischer and Neckermann, both of whom were of the German school.

I did not, in fact, see the reprise, as Ronnie Noble took me
out to Vivaro, a long wide valley overlooked by the Castel
Gandolfo, the Pope's summer palace, about fifty miles from
Rome, to see some of the three-day event dressage. Once
again no scores were announced until the end of the whole
dressage phase; even worse, between each horse, the three
judges came out of their little judging boxes and held an
earnest discussion, punctuated by much gesticulation. I
decided at Vivaro that in a three-day event it would be much
better if instead of giving competitors specific marks in the
dressage phase they were graded. A rider getting an alpha – a
good test – would start the cross-country with a bonus of, say,
50; a beta – a fair test – would carry forward a bonus of, say, 30;
a gamma – a moderate – a bonus of 20; delta, bad, 10. I still

believe that this is practical. It is ridiculous that after three days, 24 miles, and more than 40 fences a competitor can win or lose by as little as half a penalty point, at the whim of a single dressage judge.

My father's Cottage Romance, ridden by Mike Bullen, was in the British three-day event team, but unfortunately I missed his test on the Wednesday as we had had to dash back for the individual show jumping, in the Piazza di Siena; which turned out to be just about as full of drama as any Italian audience could ever desire.

At Stockholm we had the box of matches; at Rome we had the trap. The treble consisted of a big red wall, a triple bar in the middle and a set of parallels at the end. The distance between the first two parts was 23 ft 9 in, while the distance between the second two was 29 ft 6 in. For some extraordinary reason the technical delegate, Guy du Bois from Belgium, had insisted, as was his right, in altering the second distance by 6 ft. Walking the course in the early hours of the morning, which as a BBC commentator I was permitted to do, with the competitors, there was endless discussion as to whether one should take one stride or two between the last two elements; everyone knew, in fact, that a horse taking two strides would get too close to the parallels, but only a horse with exceptional scope could reach them in one. Hence the trap – and the carnage. Of the first fifteen horses, apart from Raimondo d'Inzeo on Posillipo who went clear, only one horse, Sinjon, ridden by George Morris of America had 12 faults or less. There were seven eliminations or retirements; a Belgian scored 66 – which must have pleased M du Bois! There were two scores of over 40, a number in the thirties and even d'Oriola, gold medallist in Helsinki, had 16. Most of the trouble came at this trappy treble, Fence 7.

Number sixteen to come in was David Broome on Sunsalve. Galloping round the course with tremendous élan he flew the first five fences, including the 16 ft water, just tipped the rustic poles on the turn and then sailed down to the treble. He seemed momentarily to check approaching the wall and then, unbelievably, attempted to jump the parallels with only one stride from the triple bar in the middle. He could not make it, of course, and the parallels crashed to the floor. Everyone else had tried to fit in two strides, which had been their undoing, except for Posillipo, who somehow managed it with a clever fiddle. Two fences from the end there was another little rustic fence. It was in a corner of the arena in deep shade. David seemed to come in too sharp at it and had it down, unnecessarily one felt. He took the last fence, true parallels, as if it were the last fence in a two-mile chase. It was a round of breath-taking brilliance for this young nineteen-year-old in his first Olympics.

After that it was the story as before. No more clear rounds, only cricket scores and a number of falls, all at Fence 7, including the mighty Meteor ridden by the great German ace Fritz Thiedemann, hero of so many contests, including his great duels at the White City with Alan Oliver and Red Admiral. There were eleven more eliminations. Steinkraus had 24, Goyoaga 21, Schockemohle 35¾, Favorsky, the Russian star, 28, Winkler 17, including a refusal at the treble; Pat Smythe did well to have only 20 faults, including 8 at the treble. Piero d'Inzeo achieved 8; Hugh Wiley winner of the King George V Gold Cup in 1958 and 1959 had 12.

There was a two-hour interval before the second round, and many withdrawals; in fact, only 50 per cent of the original sixty started. After a campari soda and hamburger with my producer I walked across to the practice ring in the lovely Borghese Gardens in the Piazza di Siena – surely one of the most beautiful show grounds in the world – to watch Fred Broome, David's father, riding Sunsalve. In those days Fred did all the work on the ground, just throwing David up minutes before he entered the ring, almost like a jockey in the paddock. David was standing there and I asked him if he would have somehow to negotiate a second stride between the last two elements of the treble in the second round.

'Good heavens, no', he replied. 'No problem. That wall was brand-new painted and reflecting the sun it shone like a mirror. That's why Sunsalve hesitated. This afternoon the sun will be round the other side. No problem.'

I wished him luck, but had to admit to a certain scepticism. Except for Posillipo who had 12 – he failed at the treble this time – most of those before David had scores in the twenties and thirties. Then David and Sunsalve came in. They were

going so fast after the second fence that David could not turn
Sunsalve into the third and was forced to circle it, for 3 faults.
He went down the great treble as if it were the easiest fence on
the course, with just one stride between each of the elements.
Unfortunately at the last fence of all, the big level parallels, he
stood right off again, tipping the last pole. But it was a brilliant
round for 7 faults, which could so easily have been a clear.

Piero d'Inzeo, on The Rock, managed another 8, as did
Winkler, Pat Smythe and Fritz Thiedemann each had 12; the
rest were anything between 24 and 60. David, in his first
Olympics, had won the bronze medal.

At the party at the British Embassy that evening the British
were in great form. It had just been learned that Brenda and
Little Model *were* in the top twelve of the dressage – though it
was of no avail to them – less than sixty marks behind the five
in the reprise; which considering that the top mark was 2144
was very satisfactory for a British rider. There was also news
of an excellent test by Mike Bullen and Cottage Romance at
Vivaro; but, of course, no marks. After the reception I had to
go straight to the studio to introduce the television coverage of
the individual jumping; this meant that it was well after
midnight when I reached Hotel Pacifico, but late as it was there
was no sign of my companion. When I left at 5.30 a.m. next
morning for the cross-country at Vivaro he was once again
still asleep under his sheet.

It was very close at Vivaro, even at 7.00 a.m. when the
cross-country started, but there were lowering clouds and rain
seemed likely. The course, which had always looked big, very
undulating with all the biggest fences coming towards the end
of the course, was proving more testing than expected. Only
four of the first twelve completed the course, including,
fortunately, Bertie Hill, this time riding Wild Venture on
which Laurence Rook had won a team gold at Stockholm.
Incredibly, Bertie had an almost exactly similar experience to
that which he had had on Countryman at Stockholm. As he
took off over a wide open ditch the bank gave way. Equally
incredibly, before the next horse came that part of the bank
was cordoned off, just as it had been before. As there was no
live television the BBC had a camera on a Land Rover dashing
all over the course hoping to reach a fence at the same time as a

horse – preferably a British one! When the camera whirred I spoke my commentary into an ordinary tape recorder. By cunning planning we managed to see most of Cottage Romance's round which turned out to be one of the very few clears. We were not to know then that he was penalised for being too slow on the run in; he did not realise that if he finished the cross-country early, as he did, he had to finish the whole course early. Imagining that he only had to finish within the time limit he just coasted in – and forfeited the bronze medal. In those days the 'run in' was regarded as the fifth phase and had time penalties as did the other phases. The 'run in' – usually about a hundred yards – is now incorporated into the fourth phase, the cross-country.

By now it had become obvious that the worst fences on the course were the last two. For the penultimate, huge drainpipes had been placed side by side at the top of a steep bank with only a flimsy pole in front of them. Each pipe was 7 ft long. The majority of horses obviously were frightened at being able to look through these pipes which appeared to be on the edge of a precipice. At the bottom of the bank the final fence consisted of two steep steps up on to a road, known as 'the piano', then one stride away a big rail and a bull-finch with a sizeable drop. There were appalling falls at these two fences, including Bill Roycroft of Australia who broke his arm at the pipes. One horse was destroyed, others were too lame to continue. Only 29 out of the 73 starters were fit to jump the following day; the unacceptable face of eventing, it might be said.

The final day was, in fact, something of a shambles. The jumping was due to start at 2.00 p.m. but was postponed, though whether this was because they had still failed to produce any scores, or whether it was because there was no course plan, I never discovered. (Thanks to the absence of a course plan Harry Freeman Jackson took the wrong course thus depriving the Irish team of a silver medal. At Stockholm Ian Dudgeon had eliminated the Irish team by going the wrong way on the cross-country.) Eventually the scores went up, allowing the competition to start. Australia achieved three clears to clinch their gold medal, but Bill Roycroft had to ride with his arm in a sling; there probably has never been a tougher three-day event rider than Bill – he went round

Badminton on three different horses in one day. Somehow Switzerland hung on to the silver despite Swarzenbach's score of 98¾ – Swarzenbach had won at Badminton, incidentally on Vae Victis in 1951. Both Mike Bullen and Bertie Hill had show-jumping clears, which meant that if Frank Weldon, who had had two falls on the cross-country and a stop at the pipes, had only one fence down in the show-jumping, Britain could still win the bronze. In fact he went clear, so we all sighed with relief in the knowledge that, despite the team's problems, we had not come away empty-handed; so much had been expected from us, after winning the gold in Stockholm and never since being defeated as a team. But our celebrations were premature. It was suddenly discovered that France's score had been wrongly added up. They beat us by .51 points! The *chef d'equipe*'s reaction can be imagined!

Fortunately for me there was a little light relief, though of a somewhat traumatic nature. When eventually the BBC's three-day event coverage was edited it was discovered that my tape on the cross-country pictures was blank – presumably I had pressed the wrong button, which I often do; I had, therefore, to dub a commentary on the film as it was being transmitted. I had hardly started when somewhere behind me in the studio I heard a strange thumping. A few moments later there was a terrible scream, but I dared not look round for fear of losing the place in my notes or missing something vital on the screen. Next minute, as I was commentating on a horse coming down a bank and jumping into a lake, the screen was filled with the spray as the horse landed in the water – and I was suddenly drenched. I then had to look round, to find that immediately behind me there was a little Italian 'effects' man. My tape being blank it was felt that a little local colour should be added: the thumping, a horse galloping; the scream, a horse neighing! Then when the horse jumped into the lake the little Italian, unbelievably, hurled himself, fully clothed, into a tank of water that had been brought into the studio! How I ever finished that broadcast I shall never know!

My story of this incident was the success of the delightful dinner party that evening given by Ranieri and Marie Sola Campello. Ranieri, head of the Italian motor industry, was an international show-jumping judge and often the Italian show-jumping *chef d'equipe*; Maria Sola, a charming and enthusiastic person, was heir to Fiat. Later they built the most exquisite villa in the hills above Rome, looking straight across to St Peter's. Apparently, when out hunting one day with the Rome Foxhounds Ranieri had turned to the Master, Count Alfonso Cigala Fulgosi, and informed him that he was going to build a villa on this exact site as it must have the most perfect outlook in Italy. On a later visit to Rome I had the pleasure of being entertained at the villa, but sadly just before completion Ranieri had died.

It was another late night – though I was still in bed before my companion – which was perhaps unwise in view of the very early start of the Grand Prix jumping next morning. As the event was due to start at 7.00 we had to be on the ground by 6.00. It was already extremely hot. The first horse actually appeared at 7.40 and was eliminated at 7.42. The next horse was also eliminated, while for the next eight there were scores of $25\frac{1}{2}$, 28, $50\frac{3}{4}$, $31\frac{1}{2}$ and three more eliminations. Schock-emohle made it look better with an 8, but apart from two more 8s and a 12 they were cricket scores all the way. In other words, it was a huge course; unrealistically huge.

   Sadly, one of the eliminations was Franco ridden by David Barker, as brilliant a horseman as I have ever known; two years later he was European Champion. I had the impression that the team trainer, Jack Talbot-Ponsonby, had kept this potentially brilliant combination in cotton wool, especially for the Olympics. Franco jumped superbly until reaching the treble where he stopped twice, suggesting inexperience. The last fence was coming away from the entrance and to our horror he dodged out. A quick check confirmed that elimination of one horse eliminated the whole team – it was not a case of four to jump, three to count in those days – rather than the usual adding 20 to the worst score. It was a surprise, therefore, when at the start of the second round the first horse, which had been eliminated, came in again. Frantic enquiries elicited the information that the rules had been changed: each eliminated horse would add twenty to the worst score. At least this meant that we would see our riders in action again, even if they were not in contention.

David really drove Franco round the second time for 24 faults, two of the fences down being due to flattening, going so fast. Pat Smythe, who in the first round had had 12 faults on Flanagan – a brilliant performance – now had 16. David Broome had had just three fences down in the first round, too, in the fastest time of the day; but how can one effectively describe his second round? He came in like a gladiator, swept round the course like a galleon in full sail, checked brilliantly after the water to turn at a ninety degrees angle to the big parallels which he cleared effortlessly, the first rider not to fault at either the water or the parallels, or both. In and out of the double in one huge stride, over the 5 ft 3 in wall and standing back again over the last for the only clear round of the whole event. The applause was deafening, the whole audience of 100,000 rising and cheering as David and Sunsalve left the arena.

But, as one might have suspected, it was too good to be true. The zero on the great electric score-board suddenly changed to 4. There was an angry buzz from the audience who had seen a clear round with their own eyes. Where on earth had David had 4 faults? It was not then explained, but it later transpired that the judge at the water had half-heartedly raised his flag, which the jury interpreted as a foot in the water. Exactly what happened was explained to me by Prince Bernhard of the Netherlands, then President of the International Federation, at the White City the following year. By chance, he was in the arena during Sunsalve's round. Approaching the water at such speed Sunsalve landed at least six inches clear, but with such force that he kicked some turf back into the water. Seeing the ripple, the judge at the water started to raise his flag, then had second thoughts and lowered it. At this moment apparently Prince Bernhard approached him, asking him if he knew the rules, to which, incredibly, the judge replied 'No'. The Prince explained that once a signal had been made to the jury it could not be altered without the jury's permission. It was then too late. A little disconcertingly Prince Bernhard implied that the relevance of this story was that it showed him, as FEI President, to be alert and knowledgeable, rather than that it had denied David Broome a unique clear round. Not that it was of more than academic importance in

that at the end of the competition the rules were changed yet
again. It was decided that if one member of a team was
eliminated then the whole team was eliminated. Simple
mathematics showed that had David Barker not been so
uncharacteristically eliminated Britain would certainly have
won the bronze, possibly the silver, the two lesser medals
being won by the USA and Italy with scores of 66 and 80½
respectively. For West Germany to win with a score of 46½
underlines the severity of the course.

Altogether a frustrating end to a frustrating Olympics for
Britain and for the BBC's equestrian commentator. When I
eventually reached Hotel Pacifico after two hours of traffic
jams, feeling that I had more than earned the £183.15 that I had
been paid by the BBC for my Olympic efforts, and it will be
appreciated that I was ready for a drink. Making my way to
the bar I was a little surprised to be hailed by a complete
stranger, using my Christian name; what would I like to
drink? Obviously my expression betrayed the fact that I had
no idea who it was that was kindly treating me.

'You may not recognise me', he said. 'I am Dennis
Edwards, your room companion', a film cameraman as it
turned out. Having shared a room for eight nights we shook
hands as though we were meeting each other for the first time,
which in a sense we were!

Rome International Horse Shows
When I left Rome on the Monday morning I had very little
inclination to return. To be fair, is any city at its best in the
Olympic Games? Fortunately circumstances were to lead me
back on a number of occasions, each visit increasing my
affection for the city.

My first return was the very next year. It coincided with the
Queen's visit which was to be covered for the BBC by
Richard Dimbleby. As he had gone to Moscow to cover the
May Day celebrations I was asked to stand by just in case he
was detained. Naturally, being a little anxious, I was relieved
to hear that he had arrived in Naples where the Queen was
disembarking from the Royal Yacht. However, I was asked to
remain in the Rome studio lest for some reason he was held up
on his train journey from Naples to Rome. The royal train was

due to arrive at 3.00 p.m., the broadcast starting about ten minutes earlier. The minutes ticked by and no Richard Dimbleby. 2.30, still no Richard. The producer placed in front of me a list of all the dignitaries who would be on the platform to greet the Queen. 'You'll just have to guess who is who', he said. 'At least you'll know the royal entourage.' I wished I were so confident; for some reason the BBC always seemed to assume that I moved familiarly in royal circles.

There were now less than five minutes. It was obvious that Richard was not going to make it, throwing me in at the deep end with a vengeance; though I knew Richard well enough to guess that he, wherever he was, would be as worried for me as I was for myself. Suddenly, with two minutes to go, the studio door opened and in walked Richard. Totally unflustered he sat down in front of the monitor, took from his brief-case a folder, spread out his papers in front of him and awaited the cue light. His performance was as solid, as unruffled, as reliable as ever. He identified everyone as if he had known them all his life, happily filled in when the royal train was late, appeared completely *au fait* with the formalities; the true professional.

He told us afterwards that he had had a series of appalling flights from Moscow, reaching Naples only just in time. As soon as the broadcast of the disembarking from the royal yacht was finished he was dashed by car to the station to catch his train, only to find that RAI – Italian television – had failed to appreciate that the schedules had changed on 1 May and he had therefore missed his train. The only solution was to drive him to Rome – in a mini; and Richard Dimbleby was no more a mini man than Bob Hanson.

Time-keeping has never been a noticeable quality of the Italians. Twice that week I encountered problems, once by a competition over-running due to starting an hour late, once by a competition under-running as there were no clear rounds.

On the first occasion I was commentating live for an insert into 'Grandstand'. As time passed by and the competition showed no signs of starting my BBC colleague – Alan Mouncer, a young man who was to become one of the BBC's most brilliant producers with whom I was working for the first time – was getting distraught. Finally I suggested that I might attempt to influence the show's Director, Colonel Bruno Bruni, who was walking around the arena with the course builders and other officials. I had met him at the White City and other international shows, so felt no compunction at approaching him. Recognising me he expressed great pleasure at seeing me in Rome – it was the first day of the show, the Saturday – asked me what I thought of the course, regretted that Britain had not brought a stronger team, thanked the Madonna for the good weather, hoped it would last all the following week and again welcomed me. At last I managed to make my point: was it not possible to start the competition? Why? he enquired. I explained that the competition, the start of which was an hour overdue, was being transmitted to BBC's 'Grandstand'.

'Television!' he exclaimed. 'We do not put ourselves out for television. Do you know what RAI pay for this show, the whole eight days? Just 70,000 lira' (about £300). I felt that there was little point in telling him that the BBC had only paid £300 for the first Horse of the Year Show.

Fortunately the competition was under way in about ten minutes, but before very long I rather wished that it were not. I had just commentated on a good round by Ireland's Billy Ringrose when Raimondo d'Inzeo came in on a great Irish horse, The Quiet Man, one of his two mounts in the Grand Prix. Having started late the authorities were at least trying to make up time, so the judges were being very quick on the starting bell. I was just completing what I had to say about d'Inzeo – his gold medal in the previous year's Olympics, in this very stadium, the background to his horse – when wham! I was struck by a really heavy blow on the back of the head. Astonished, and apprehensive, I looked round to find the spectators all gesticulating wildly and ssh-ing. (My commentary position was just a little table in the middle of the open stand on the south side.)

'What the hell –?' I started. Alan Mouncer leapt to his feet and faced them. After a few hectic whispers he sat down. Apparently, he told me, the Italian spectators do not allow anyone to talk while a d'Inzeo is jumping: hence the whack with a heavy rolled-up newspaper. I carried on with Alan

Mouncer standing guard behind me. When the next rider came in, the British entry, General Monkey Blacker on Workboy, I turned round and said ssh! as the spectators started talking, which was not greatly appreciated; but later I received apologies both from RAI and from the show organisers.

The Grand Prix was brought forward to the Wednesday as the Queen was to visit the show that day. The BBC was covering the Queen's arrival and the barrage (jump-off) live at what would be about 6.00 p.m. in England. The competition, for once, started more or less punctually at 2.30 p.m., but it was a big course which proved surprisingly difficult. It soon became obvious that there would never be the expected ten or twelve clear rounds, possibly none at all. It became equally obvious that the whole competition would be over before ever the Queen arrived. Again, as our transmission time approached, Alan Mouncer asked me to tackle Bruno Bruni. On this occasion he was a little more sympathetic, as for the competition to be finished before the Queen's arrival would be, to say the least, ridiculous, not to say discourteous. Eventually with just four clears it was decided to hold an interval before the jump-off. The Queen duly arrived. As soon as the introductions were completed she settled down to watch the jump-off between Raimondo d'Inzeo on his Olympic gold medallist, Posillipo, 'Monkey' Blacker on Workboy, Billy Ringrose with his two horses, Loch an Easpaig and Cloyne: just the four. In six minutes it was all over with Ringrose finishing first and second, achieving without doubt the greatest success of his career. Our transmission under-ran by about twenty minutes which was not very popular with 'presentation' at Lime Grove.

'Monkey' Blacker, who at the end of 1984 finished his four-year term as President of the British Equestrian Federation, was leading the British team in Rome in 1961. 'Zulu', his wife, was with him and they kindly asked me to accompany them on a sight-seeing tour. As they were familiar with Rome, while for me it was my first visit (apart from the Olympics when there had been no opportunity for sight-seeing), it was very helpful, though we never managed to see St Peter's, hoping to fit it in on another day; a pious hope as it turned out. But for one whose great love for the plays of Shakespeare stemmed from a study of *Julius Caesar* at school it was an unforgettable experience to find oneself standing on the actual flags where Caesar had been struck down by the conspirators nearly two thousand years earlier.

Two years later when again the BBC sent me out to cover the show Jennifer came with me. The weather, unfortunately, was appalling; so bad in fact that the show was cancelled two days running – at least enabling us to visit St Peter's – which meant that it finished two days late. Despite the discomfort of sitting in my open-air commentary box under incessant rain we thoroughly enjoyed our week, with Alan Mouncer, especially our evening at the Campello villa; but the delay did cause problems as we had arranged to join friends in Spain for a holiday. Eventually, three days later than intended, we made our way to Marbella by a somewhat circuitous route via Madrid, Barcelona and Malaga. There was a three-hour delay in Barcelona, which enabled us to buy an English paper in which we read of the famous train robbery – only five miles from our home at Pendley. Indeed, it was to the cottage of the father of a great friend of ours, John Rawdin, an outstanding personality in the horse world, that the wretched, stricken train driver staggered.

Oddly enough, on the day before we flew out to Rome I was driving with my then four-year-old daughter, Carola, to the Whaddon Chase Kennels at Wing, when I noticed in a field a small single-engine aeroplane, less than a mile from the bridge where the train was stopped. Thinking it would amuse Carola to see it at closer quarters I stopped the car by the gate. But as we entered the field a man who had apparently been studying a map saw us and, climbing into the plane, immediately flew off. It seemed so possible that the pilot was planning the route from the bridge to their hide-out at Letherslade Farm, near Bicester, that when I arrived home I reported it to Brigadier Cheyney, a friend of mine who was then Chief Constable. When the train robbers were caught I hoped that the Brigadier might advise me to claim the £100,000 reward – but he never did!

My next visit to Rome, in 1969, for television might easily

have been a complete fiasco. As it was it had its farcical moments. The trip being arranged at very short notice for some reason we had no hotel accommodation booked in advance. Geoff Goddard from the BBC flew out a day early, but when he met me at the airport he told me that as it was horse show week and the beginning of the tourist season he had had great difficulty in getting any rooms at all. Finally he had booked us in at – yes, none other than the Excelsior on the Via Veneto. Naturally I was delighted. The BBC does not usually accommodate its commentators at five-star hotels. There was just one snag: it being the week of May Day most Italian workers, many of whom have communist sympathies, were inevitably on strike. The Excelsior could serve no meals; we had to make our own beds; if we wanted breakfast we could fetch coffee and rolls from the hotel kitchen. Fortunately the bar was in operation. As there was no public transport Geoff had hired a car, which proved to be extremely necessary although the Piazza di Siena is just at the top of the Via Veneto. Inevitably when we arrived at the show ground next day we were informed that as from midnight all RAI employees would be on strike, which meant that although we would be able to cover the Grand Prix that afternoon, we would not be able to televise the event that we had really come for, the Olgiata. This event, similar to the Hamburg Derby or Hickstead Derby, staged in the grounds of a very fine country club some miles out of Rome, was almost more like a cross-country course than a show-jumping course. It had been a great success the previous year and now Anneli Drummond Hay had been sent out specifically to win it on Merely-a-Monarch. The event was to be a main feature of BBC's 'Sportsnight', whose editor was not at all pleased to hear of the cancelled transmission; although I doubt if when despairingly he appealed to Geoff Goddard to 'do something' he expected Geoff to take him quite so literally – but Geoff is certainly not lacking in initiative.

As soon as we returned to the hotel he was on the telephone. An hour later he was on his way to the airport, instructing me to remain in Rome until he returned on Friday, which allowed me two very pleasant days on my own in Rome with nothing to do. To my astonishment when he arrived back he had with him three cameramen and three cameras. All he had to do was to get permission to televise the event unilaterally; in other words the BBC would do it, but no one else would, as all others were dependent upon the RAI pictures. This, of course, was not going to be too easy as it might be regarded as a form of strike breaking and could well be 'blacked'. The RAI director was happy to turn a blind eye, but should any of those on strike discover what was happening there would be real trouble. We went out to the club where Geoff, having inspected the site, had decided that there were sufficient suitable positions which, if they did not wholly conceal the cameramen, could at least enable them to look like spectators with their private ciné cameras. There was also a convenient bush where I could sit with a little picnic and a hidden microphone.

When the show's President, Count Enrico Buschetti, heard what was happening he immediately asked me to meet him. I knew him quite well as he had often judged in England. He had a problem, he told me. His sponsor for the Olgiata – Johnson's (baby powder) – had pulled out as the competition was not now being televised; but he hoped that they might be satisfied if they knew that the BBC was televising it, their product being no less in demand in Britain than in Italy. What size audience did 'Sportsnight' have? he asked. About twelve million I told him, making a guess. That sounded good enough, he thought, more than in all Italy; he would contact Johnson's immediately. That evening he rang me at my hotel to inform me that his sponsors were happy and would honour their sponsorship. He was sure that the television would be a success. He was profuse with his thanks.

It was a glorious day for the Olgiata, a beautiful setting, a large crowd, a top-class international field. Anneli Drummond Hay duly won on Merely-a-Monarch; it made memorable television. Our under-cover operation – almost literally under cover – had worked perfectly. Enrico Buschetti was delighted, 'Sportsnight' was delighted. I was happy; Geoff, justifiably, having master-minded the whole operation, was like a dog with two tails, insisting that he take me out for a really expensive dinner at one of the best restaurants in Rome – all, we hoped, at the BBC's expense. When I collected my key from the hotel there was a large envelope in my locker. It was an invitation from the President to the official show lunch at the smart country club the next day, Sunday. In his own hand Enrico had written on the invitation 'Please bring your crew'. Geoff was thrilled, knowing the pleasure that it would give his cameramen whom he immediately telephoned, telling them to postpone their return to England until Monday.

As Geoff's hired car was only a mini he said that he would run me up to the club early – the invitation was for 11.30 a.m., lunch 12.30 p.m.: the final performance of the show starting at 3.00 a.m. – then go back for the crew. Enrico Buschetti, very tall and elegant, greeted me most warmly, seeming genuinely grateful that we had helped him solve his problem. As the guests arrived, it soon became obvious that this was a very smart, social occasion, typical of a Roman Sunday. In due course a coachload arrived, bringing the international teams, all in smart blazers or uniforms, which explained why each table, except the top tables, had a national flag on it. Geoff Goddard and his team had still not arrived when the elegant company – uniforms, neat grey suits, silk ties, smart hats for the few ladies, with expensive jewellery and gloves – began to drift towards the tables for luncheon. Apart from the seven or eight tables with flags for the teams there was a top table and three or four other smaller tables. As each table fairly quickly became filled I thought I had better ask Enrico where I and the BBC team should sit. For a moment he seemed non-plussed, then looking around he said 'Ah, yes! the Swiss are not here. You can sit at their table', which was right in the middle of the room. Everyone was seated, lunch was about to be served, when Geoff and the cameramen arrived. Geoff was suitably attired in a lightweight suit; but the cameramen – jeans, anoraks, moccasin shoes, open-neck shirts, two in peaked caps. One could not blame them; they had not expected to be invited to a smart, social occasion – they had just come at very short notice to do a job. But I could happily have disappeared through the floor, while I had a feeling that Enrico might well be regretting his kind invitation. I rather doubt if he had ever encountered a television camera crew at close quarters before.

Worse was to come. Having finished our first course, an exquisite prawn cocktail, made all the more succulent by the

Soave Classico which was served with it, we had just made our way to the great buffet table from which we were to help ourselves to a host of magnificent cold viands, when I looked round and saw to my horror that our table was now occupied – by the Swiss! Nobody else, other than Geoff and his crew, seemed to notice our dilemma. I had no alternative but to seek out Enrico again, now in the centre of the top table. This time he was really non-plussed, and for a few minutes was completely lost for words, muttering under his breath in Italian. Fortunately the head waiter soon came to our rescue arranging for his assistants to set up an extra table – in the annexe, where, I have to admit, everyone, including myself, felt very much more at ease. Once settled down we all enjoyed our splendid society lunch to the full; an experience which, I have no doubt, was remembered and talked about by the camera crew for a long time.

I made one final visit to Rome in the late seventies, a year or two before I retired from the BBC. It was a brief visit, but it all went without a hitch. The Borghese Gardens seemed more beautiful than ever. To sit outside a little bar on the Via Veneto and watch the world pass by was no less entertaining than on my first visit. To peep through the front entrance of the Hotel Excelsior brought back many memories – both of smoked salmon sandwiches and champagne and making my own coffee in the kitchen. I had, in fact, grown very fond of Rome.

Chapter 3

Viva Mexico

Tokyo, 1964

To visit Rome these days is not, for the average person, very unusual. It is very much more rare to have the opportunity to go to Tokyo. For this reason I was particularly pleased to know that the 1964 Olympics were to be held in Japan, realising that I was likely to be a member of the BBC's television team. There was a personal involvement again for me in that my father had a horse in the team, Sea Breeze, which was to be ridden by Michael Bullen. He had also trained Richard Meade who, on Barbery, was riding in his first Olympics. Never having been to the Far East I was really looking forward to it.

But it was not to be. I was all set to leave on the Sunday morning after the last night of the Horse of the Year Show; indeed, I had arranged a 5.00 a.m. call on the telephone to enable me to pack and get to the airport. It was, however, at 3.00 a.m. that I was awoken on the telephone. It was Peter Dimmock, head of the BBC's Olympic squad in Tokyo. They had lost the sound in Tokyo; a severed cable or something. There was no point in my going to Tokyo; I would have to commentate 'off the tube', as it is called – in other words, commentate on a picture on a monitor set in a studio in London. Further, I was told that there would be only two transmissions: one commentary would be on a twenty-minute pull-together of the three-day event, and one on a forty-minute live television broadcast from the show jumping, using a guide line commentator, which means that one is in permanent contact by television with someone on the site who identifies, gives one scores and so on, there being no sound. As the picture turned out to be very indistinct and the guide-line

commentator a Frenchman who did not speak English and had
never previously watched show jumping, it was not one of my
most satisfying broadcasts. Fortunately I had not forgotten the
advice that I was given when first I became a commentator:
'when in doubt, say nowt'. I was, however, much amused
when out riding, early the next morning, to be asked by an old
lady if I had come over by satellite, as she had heard me in
Tokyo the night before.

Though this second-hand communication was very
unsatisfactory, on top of the disappointment at not being
there, nevertheless as the news began to filter through I began
to feel almost relieved that I was not in Tokyo. At the end of
the cross-country phase of the three-day event Richard Meade
on Barbery was, doubtless to my father's delight, in the lead
with a score of 65.67, but then had a disastrous round in the
show jumping, collecting some 36 faults which dropped him
down to eighth, one ahead of Sergeant Ben Jones on Master
Barnard, who himself had 30 faults on Master Barnard;
apparently a number of fences had false groundlines. Sea
Breeze had had a fall on the steeplechase course, Mike Bullen
breaking his arm. I learned later that he had over-jumped. He
was an exceptionally bold jumper, as I well know having had
four wonderful seasons hunting on him after he had retired,
but he had this tendency to over-jump, as he did at Burghley
the following year, when his fall probably cost him first prize.
One day out hunting with me he jumped so big that he landed
in an old domestic bath that the farmer was using as a water
trough. It turned him over, but fortunately we were both
unscathed. At Tokyo he should not really have been allowed
to start the cross-country with Mike Bullen having a broken
arm; but when it was heard that our fourth rider, James
Templer on M'Lord Connolly, had gone off at a quite unreal-
istic speed, considering the appalling going – does it always
rain the night before the cross-country in an Olympic three-
day event? – and then, three fences from home, had run out of
steam and was eliminated, it was obvious that Mike and Sea
Breeze would have to do the cross-country if Britain was to
continue as a team; in the three-day event it was four to start
with three to count as, after Mexico, it was with the show
jumping. Unfortunately having gone brilliantly round three

quarters of the course Sea Breeze missed his footing at a bank and slipped back into the ditch and could not get out. This eliminated the team – a bitter disappointment for all involved. I was glad to be spared the disappointment.

The show jumping was not much better. With the Games coming so late in the year – mid-October – most of our 'possibles' had been over-jumped, were stale or lame. It was scarcely, therefore, a representative team that went to Tokyo. David Broome on the old warrior, Jacopo, once a successful show hunter, had 16 and 12 faults respectively; in the first round, young David Boston Barker, a distant cousin of the David Barker who had been in the team in Rome, riding Northern Light, started with 28½, recovering a little in the second round with 16. Only Peter Robeson with 8 in each round excelled, winning the bronze medal after a jump-off against John Fahey of Australia. Again, something of a let-down one felt; and again a certain relief at not being present in person. Being almost too patriotic by nature, often becoming too involved, perhaps, with the performance of British riders – which led sometimes to commentaries less detached than they should have been – I always feel a British failure deeply, just as I swell with pride, as if it were all my own effort, when I see the Union Jack raised and hear the British national anthem played; as, of course, I did in Mexico in 1968.

Mexico, 1968

As perhaps I should have anticipated in that exciting country, the Mexico Olympics had a dramatic start as far as I was concerned. The afternoon after my arrival I had instructions to meet in the foyer of my hotel an official of the BBC who would take me down to the Olympic Press Centre where I would pick up my accreditation papers and badges. I had been warned that the standard of driving in Mexico was nothing if not alarming, and further that the university students who had been employed to drive the courtesy cars, of which a number were allotted to the BBC, drove like maniacs. When, in 1962, Mexico had applied for the 1968 Olympics they had conveniently forgotten to mention the storms that hit the city without fail at 2.00 p.m. precisely every afternoon. Day after day the tracks events in the Olympic stadium were interrupted

by torrential downpours. It was in just such a downpour that
we set off for the Press Centre. Driving along one of the tree-
fringed boulevards the rain was so heavy that it must have
been almost impossible for the driver to see. In fact, the
likelihood is that he did not see. Approaching traffic lights the
cars in front of us stopped, probably rather abruptly. As the
driver applied the brakes of our car we went into a skid. The
next moment we crashed into the car in front of us. Not very
seriously, but unfortunately the car behind then banged into
us, at about fifty miles an hour. The next thing I knew was that
I was lying on the floor of the car in a pool of blood; for a
second or two I did not realise that it was my own blood – in
fact, I hardly realised anything at all. The next moment, dazed
and bewildered, I found myself being seized by one arm and
the collar of my coat and pulled out of the car into the road,
where for a moment or two I was left lying. Before I could
understand what was happening I was lugged off the road into
another vehicle by the curb, then collapsed on the seat, blinded
by the blood pouring from a wound in my scalp.

Gradually pulling myself together I asked what was happening. The driver, it seemed, had explained to my BBC
colleague that in Mexico if one was involved in an accident one
had to get away from it as quickly as possible, angry drivers
being inclined to draw a gun on anyone they believed to be
responsible for the accident. Indeed, at the very moment of
my little drama none other than General Humberto Mariles
Cortes, the show-jumping gold medal winner in 1948, was
languishing in gaol, where he had been committed since 1966
for shooting, and killing, the driver of a car with which he was
involved in an accident. Harry Llewellyn, a member of the
International Federation at that time, did everything in his
power to get him released so that he could watch the show
jumping, but to no avail; in fact, he died in gaol some years
later. I had no wish to be the unwitting cause of anyone being
committed to a Mexican prison.

By the time that we had reached the Press Centre, found the
right department and downed a strong brandy I was more or
less myself again. They patched up my head in the first-aid
room, but it was the mess that my smart new lightweight coat
was in that distressed me most – it was ruined, though I am

glad to say that eventually the BBC compensated me. It can be imagined what I looked like in my passport-type photograph for my accreditation card. I kept it for a long time to convince those who found it difficult to believe my story that I was telling the truth. They could see for themselves the congealed blood on my brow and my matted hair.

I do not know why the BBC arranged for me to go out to Mexico quite so early. There was a full week before the equestrian events commenced. As only rarely was it possible for me to get a ticket for the athletics, or indeed any other event, I found myself very much on my own. I was, in fact, the only 'specialist' commentator. All the rest of the team, being on the staff of the BBC, were expected to turn their hands to anything. As it was a comparatively small team it meant that everyone was fully occupied, recording during the day and dubbing and transmitting through the evening until late at night; everyone, that is, except me. Leading such a full and busy life at home I began to feel very much at a loose end. By lunch-time I had usually 'done' the sights that I had earmarked for that day. To go far afield presented problems in that taxis, if available, were very expensive and one's money limited, and I had no car alotted to me personally. I spent much time, therefore, walking around the city, superficially beautiful and impressive, but, just one street away from the main boulevardes, there were depravity, appalling poverty and squalor, large families or communities living in filthy shacks, waif-like children in rags imploring one for money. It was a depressing experience; but, of course, one was helpless, other than the few pesetas one could give the children. Fortunately, though with a certain guilty embarrassment, I found one or two charming little French restaurants, intimate, dimly lit, with superb cuisine, and quite inexpensive. To these I used to repair each evening, with my paperback and cigar. Here, indeed, was contentment; but I would have appreciated a companion.

One evening, returning to my hotel to watch the Games on television, I discovered, to my annoyance, that my set would not work. It had been perfectly all right the evening before, but now it was dead. I phoned down to the hall porter; there was no one who could help. Reception informed me that the

engineer was off duty. Hearing a lot of noise in the room next
to mine, which happened to be David Coleman's, just at the
time that the event I particularly wanted to see was due, I
decided to go in, as I felt sure that those with David would be
wanting to watch too, as they were. I received a warm
welcome and was quickly regaled with a drink from the
special bar installed in David's, and only David's, room.
When I explained that my set had broken down I was assured
that I was welcome to watch David's television at any time:
my key, he assured me, would fit his lock. He had discovered
that all the locks were the same! When the transmission was
over, everyone had another drink, eventually departing to
their own rooms. As I was about to leave David stopped me,
asking me to hold on a minute. As soon as we were alone he
told me that he had a confession to make. It was his television
that had broken down, so he had 'borrowed' mine! I stayed
and chatted for half an hour or so and discovered what a very
likeable, human, sensitive person David is. At that time he had
something of a reputation for being arrogant, brusque and
over-riding, demanding anything and everything. I did not
find him like that. If he wanted a greater control of the
situation than commentators usually have, then, it seemed to
me, he was justified in demanding it as he had an efficiency and
ability that was quite remarkable, and I am sure still is. Perhaps
I was sympathetic in that when show jumping and eventing
were first televised the producers were entirely ignorant of
equestrian sports, which made me feel justified in demanding a
certain amount of control over the transmission. David kindly
arranged tickets for me to watch the 100 metres heats the
following morning. That evening I watched the recording. He
covered twenty-one heats in succession, during which he
never made a single error. It was one of the most brilliantly
professional performances that I can recall. I was glad to have
had the opportunity to get to know David better. If nothing
else it made my visit to Mexico worthwhile. I have tended,
almost inevitably, though not deliberately, to remain a little
aloof from my fellow commentators whom I always regarded
as very much more professional than myself. For each of them
it was his whole life. It was only a part of mine.

The BBC's Head of Sport in Mexico obviously had so

much on his plate that he had not, apparently, appreciated the fact that Avandoro, the venue for the three-day event, was nearly 100 miles from Mexico City. As he was so fully occupied it was difficult for me to elicit any hard and fast plans from him. Eventually, however, I persuaded him to make a car available to drive me down to Avandoro on 19 October, the second day of the three-day event dressage, but was told that I would have to fix up my own accommodation as it would be impossible for me to have a car to drive all that distance four days running. I was not too sure that I wanted one in any case – my experience of driving in Mexico so far not being encouraging – but knowing all too well the pressure on accommodation at an Olympic event, I was somewhat apprehensive. Raymond Brooks-Ward, who was in Mexico for BBC Radio, heard that I was going and asked for a lift. Officially radio was only covering the show jumping, but he felt that it might be useful to be at Avandoro.

We drove through beautiful scenery down the Toluca Morelia highway before turning down a valley of even more dramatically impressive scenery, finally reaching Valle de Bravo and the Avandoro Golf Club, where the event was to be held, in the early evening. Our first job was to find the Press Centre, which was situated in a charming little wooden building surrounded by a moat. As we arrived the Centre was teeming with the whole world's equestrian press, the first day's dressage having just been completed. As I descended the steps an old friend, Hans Ulrich Eisenbach, senior German commentator, turned, and seeing me, exclaimed 'Ah! Here at last we have the pillar of England!' which brought roars of laughter, but a very warm welcome. What my friend meant was that the doyen of English commentators had now arrived, I, of course, having been a commentator longer than anyone else; since 1948, in fact, as far as the Olympic Games were concerned.

Having completed the formalities we enquired about accommodation. We were directed to a special desk where a harrassed Mexican gentleman was attempting to cope with the apparently hopeless task of finding accommodation for a horde of journalists who had come, like Raymond and myself, without making any previous arrangements. The situation

looked pretty desperate until suddenly the gimlet-eyed
Raymond spotted my name at the top of the list on the
official's desk. Oh yes, we were informed, the BBC had
booked accommodation over a year earlier – and had
obviously forgotten. We were given the name of my hotel and
cadged a lift there from another commentator.

It was an exquisitely beautiful hotel by the side of a broad
stream. Fortunately I had been allotted a double room – in fact,
it had three beds in it – so Raymond found himself fixed up
too. Our room on the ground floor looked out on a magnificent waterfall which fell so close to the window that if we left it
open all our clothes were damp from the spray.

That evening we were invited to a reception given by Prince
Philip. On returning to the hotel I was informed by the hotel
porter that unfortunately they had had to put a third person
into our room. He was sure that I would not be
inconvenienced as the third bed was behind a curtain. Our
dormitory mate, apparently, was a Roman Catholic priest
who was covering the equestrian events for a Mexican paper:
interesting and unusual! The gentleman was not in the room
when I retired to bed, but in the middle of the night I woke up
to find, to my alarm, that Father X was sitting on my bed.
From his behaviour and remarks when he realised that I was
awake I decided that firm action was required. Sitting up in
bed I forcibly pushed him away from me, calling across as he
retired behind his curtain:

'You stay there, Father; and please remember that although
you may be a holy father, I am a real father', adding 'and
what's more I have photographs of my children to prove it.'

Next morning I told Raymond of my experience, but to our
relief we had no further trouble. Truly Mexico was turning
out to be nothing if not interesting.

We were up early on cross-country day. Someone kindly
gave us a lift to the steeplechase course, which was high up in
the hills and more like a cross-country course with solid walls,
massive poles and big ditches. They were certainly formidable, but after the first three horses over the steeplechase had all
picked up bonus points I felt happier about the chances of our
first horse and rider, Lochinvar and Derek Allhusen. Sure
enough, they too collected bonus points – 35.2 to be precise.

Jane Bullen on little Our Nobby did even better, scoring the maximum 37.6; though sadly an hour later, watching from the score-board on the Los Espinos plateau, I was to see her fall at some comparatively inocuous water on the cross-country. Despite this, however, Britain was far from out of it, the cross-country taking the anticipated heavy toll, especially amongst the less experienced teams. After the first two from each team had gone there had not been many eliminations but many scores had reached more than 100 penalty points. Richard Meade, third to go for Britain, on Cornishman V, was on the steeplechase course at about 1.00 p.m., picking up the maximum bonus, but as he completed his second roads and tracks ominous black clouds were rolling up over the mountains and thunder could be heard in the distance. As he started the cross-country I felt the first heavy drop of rain. I looked at my watch: sure enough it was two o'clock.

As I made my way towards a big set of rails with a ditch in front, about three quarters of the way round the course, where I had hoped to see Richard Meade I put on my plastic mac, pushing my field glasses into the pocket. By the time I reached the fence tropical rain was falling in stair-rods. There was dramatic lightning and thunder. I actually heard Cornishman approaching the fence before I could see him. How he jumped it, effortlessly, despite the take-off being invisible, I shall never know, but he did and carried on, disappearing into the holocaust. By the time I reached the end of the course I might just as well have had no clothes on at all: I was literally soaked to the skin, while the lenses of my glasses were waterlogged – so much so, in fact, that they were unusable for the rest of my stay in Mexico.

Richard, I was told, had successfully completed the course a few minutes earlier, but the whole of the last part of the course was now flooded; in fact, the floodwater stretched fifty yards either side of the running stream that was a feature of the end of the course. Would they not have to abandon the event? The final complex, approached across a short plateau, consisted of a rivetted bank the far side of the stream which was here chanelled through wooden boards; circling left horses had then to re-cross the stream by jumping into a ford. With the flooding it was, of course, impossible again to see the take-off

before the bank, yet somehow the last few riders, who
suffered worst from the conditions, brilliantly persuaded their
horses to take off on the correct stride. The return over the
stream, however, presented greater problems, the stream
being so swollen, the current now so fast, that almost inevitably, if a horse dropped in direct, rather than slithering down
the bank at an angle, its legs were swept from under it. Two
horses were carried away by the raging torrent, one struggling
to its feet 100 yards down stream, the other stopped by a
branch that some stewards had pulled across the stream; but
this, of course, acted as a dam which worsened the situation,
by increasing the depth of the stream at the point of entry.
Fortunately after a few minutes the branch itself was swept
away by the swirling, frothing water, the colour of rust.

I cannot remember who suggested it or who was the leader.
It seemed suddenly just to happen. First a couple of spectators
leapt into the stream; others immediately followed, including,
goodness knows why, myself. We linked arms, standing hip
to hip, waiting for the next horse. When it arrived and was
swept towards us we were able to prevent it going any further
and helped it up the bank. The same thing happened with the
next horse. By now people were rushing up and down
demanding, in a wide variety of languages, that the whole
event be halted; there was, in fact – and, indeed, not surprisingly – considerable hysteria, which could easily have led to
the whole situation getting out of hand. Fortunately the
technical delegate, Laurence Rook, who had been in Britain's
gold-medal team in Stockholm twelve years earlier, was on
the spot or arrived as soon as the trouble was reported to him.
To stop the event or to continue was his responsibility, and his
alone. Catching sight of me in the stream he shouted at me to
come out. I was happy to obey him.

'We are going to carry on', he said. He had made up his
mind, but wanted assurance and support. I told him that
despite the ugly atmosphere that seemed to be developing I
was sure that he was right. The rain had stopped; there were
only about eight more horses to go, the better ones ridden by
the most experienced riders, going last for their team. Even in
all the excitement and chaos I was convinced that if the cross-
country were called off now it would not only be the last time

1a. Official arm-badge: all that was required to allow me to any part of Wembley Stadium or Olympic Village in 1948. Security seemed non-existent in those carefree days.

1b. Our first visit to South Africa coincided with 'Sharpeville', but it was not allowed to affect the relaxed atmosphere of the Rand Show – at which one was expected to judge just about everything.

2a. Countryman III, owned by the Queen and ridden by Bertie Hill, straddled across the famous trakhener (Fence 22) at the Stockholm Olympics. Bertie Hill can be seen trying to propel his horse forward over the pole, before the arrival of Colonel Cox-Cox, who advised the opposite.

2b. The three-day event gold medallists at Stockholm, 1956. From left, Major Frank Weldon on his own Kilbarry, Bertie Hill on Countryman and Major Laurence Rook on P. E. Marsh's Wild Venture.

3a. Little Model, owned and ridden by Mrs V. D. S. (Brenda) Williams, the 'galloping grandma', representing Britain in the dressage at the Rome Olympics in 1960.

3b. David Broome on Mr Anderson's Sunsalve wins the individual bronze in the show jumping at the Rome Olympics.

4a. Anneli Drummond-Hay on her way to winning the Olgiata – the show-jumping Derby – on Xanthos in 1970, having won it the previous year on Merely-a-Monarch.

4b. The gothic cathedral at Aachen in Germany, the old capital of Charlemagne's Europe, now another famous centre of show-jumping.

5a. Mexico's magnificent Olympic Stadium.

5b. Marion Coakes (now Mould) on Stroller at the start of their round in the individual show-jumping event which won her the silver medal. Bill Steinkraus won the gold on Snowbound, David Broome the bronze on Mister Softee.

6a. Captain Mark Phillips on Great Ovation towards the end of the three-day event cross-country course at the Munich Olympics in 1972. The rein which was broken at his fall at Fence 4 is looped over his horse's nose. Clear in the show jumping, he was a member of Britain's gold-medal-winning team.

6b. Kevin Freeman on Good Mixture (USA) negotiating the awkward sunken-road fence. Colonel Frank Weldon, the British team trainer, can be seen watching in the background, just to the right of the tree.

7a. Ann Moore on Psalm on her way to the jump–off which won her the silver medal at the Munich Olympics.

7b. Nymphenburg Palace, the beautiful venue for the Olympic dressage in 1972.

8a. The beautifully set-out dressage arena at Bromont for the Montreal Olympics of 1976.

8b. Alwin Schockemohle jumping the final fence on Warwick to clinch the gold medal with the only clear. A minute later the heavens opened, postponing the jump-off for silver and bronze.

that a three-day event was included in the Olympic Games, but it would be a devastating blow for a sport which already had its critics.

Laurence was proved right. Bill Roycroft of Australia, Horst Karsten of Germany, Michael Plumb of the USA, Evdokimov of Russia, Ben Jones for Britain, all came through unscathed. The protesters began to feel that they had, perhaps, been premature in wanting the event abandoned, even that they could be labelled 'chicken'. Everyone, in fact, afterwards, seemed anxious to let one know that they had been all for carrying on. It has to be admitted, however, that though being present at what were surely the most dramatic moments in any three-day event anywhere, yet it was an experience that one would never wish to repeat. There was something almost Wagnerian about it: the storm, the drama, the climax – and there could so easily have been tragedy too.

At the end of the second day Britain had a commanding lead which they maintained in the sodden show-jumping arena the following day, to win the gold medal by nearly fifty points from West Germany, with Australia third. But here there really was tragedy, although it was a Russian rider who was involved, not a British. In the lead for the individual was the French rider Guyon on Pitou with a total of −28.61, but hard on his heels were James Wofford, USA, on Kilkenny, −30.31, Pavel Deev, Russia, on Packet −37.91, and Derek Allhusen, Britain, on Lochinvar, −40.61. Guyon had a fence down and time faults to bring his total to −38.86. He could now be beaten either by Wofford or Deev; but Wofford had a disastrous round with three fences down and time faults. Deev only had to go clear to win. The suspense was tremendous. He seemed to take the earlier part of the course faster than the others – most earlier riders had collected time faults in the heavy going – so with two fences to go time faults at least were out of the question, but then, unbelievably – he took the wrong course! The bell rang, he looked round and pulled up. For a moment he sat there, seemingly stunned, then throwing the reins on his horse's neck he buried his face in his hands. After what seemed like minutes he picked up his reins, spurred his horse to an instant gallop and dashed out of the ring. The story goes that he galloped straight through the collecting ring, up into the hills beyond the Valley of the Brave, never to be seen again. Presumably he found the Mexican mountains preferable to Siberian steppes.

For the record, Derek Allhusen, on Lochinvar, jumped a clear round with no time faults, giving him the individual silver.

If there was drama in the three-day event there was certainly a touch of farce too. On the second roads-and-tracks phase of the cross-country one of the riders – we will just refer to him as a member of a commonwealth team – was descending a narrow path through a wood when suddenly a little man – allegedly connected with one of the Eastern block teams – leapt out from behind a bush brandishing a syringe. He was about to plunge it in the neck of the commonwealth rider's horse when he received a sharp crack across his hand from the commonwealth rider's whip. Jumping back, he looked up, murmured 'Sorry, wrong horse!' and disappeared into the shrubbery. But whether it was the intention of the little man allegedly connected with an Eastern block team to boost the performance of an ally or to damage the chances of a rival will never be known.

After four exhausting days at Avandoro one was grateful for a day's respite before the individual show jumping, which was at Campo Marto, a park some way from the centre of the city. Here we had the unforgettable thrill of seeing Marion Mould on her remarkable pony, Stroller, achieve one of the only two clear rounds in the first round. The second round had one of the biggest fences that I have ever seen: true parallels 5 ft 3 in with a 7 ft spread. It was just too much for Stroller, as indeed it was for every single horse in the second round. One fence catching everyone out was a unique experience in the Olympic Games; even Bill Steinkraus on Snowbound faulted here. Sadly, Stroller had a pole down at the last double as well, so Steinkraus won the gold, Stroller the silver and David Broome, on Mister Softee, the bronze, after a jump-off with five others, including Chapot of the United States, which was a very satisfactory start for Britain.

The real drama, however, was in the team event three days later. It was a huge course, with a double of rustic poles, true again, 4 ft 10 in high, 5 ft 6 in wide, 24 ft 6 in apart, coming just 28 yards – at most eight strides – from 16 ft of open water; but even more formidable was the treble, Fence 6, with a 5 ft 3 in red wall in, parallel poles at 4 ft 9 in by 5 ft 4 in in the middle and then 6 ft wide parallel poles, 5 ft high: 34 ft between the first two elements, 24 ft between the second two. After so much rain the going had made the course particularly demanding. The first round for Britain was encouraging. Stroller, going first, faulted at the middle part of the treble and then both elements of the big double after the water; Harvey Smith on Madison Time had 18½ faults, including the double; David Broome on Mister Softee had a wonderful round for 8, which took Britain into the lead at the end of the first round with a score of 48, ahead of Canada, 49½, and France 56½. The severity of the course is underlined by the fact that Germany, Italy and the USA all had scores of over 60.

There had been much controversy before the event about the dropping of The Maverick and Alison Dawes from the team when they had been brought out especially as a team combination, Stroller only being earmarked for the individual. But how could Stroller be left out having won the silver, even if he was suffering from an abscess in his mouth? Now after the first round he was right up with the leaders.

My experience has been that horses always jump better in the second round of a team event, the fences being familiar. Similarly it is comparatively seldom that horses have a fence down in a jump-off, despite the fact that they are going very fast over big fences. I was confident, therefore, that our riders would improve on their performance in the second round at Mexico; indeed, it seemed to me that had we no more than the luck we were entitled to a gold was within our grasp. Perhaps, almost subconsciously, I felt a pang of apprehension when I saw that Stroller was sweating as he came in. I could not remember him sweating so profusely on any previous occasion. Could he be suffering from his tooth? It seemed ominous, too, that the first seven before Stroller all had worse scores than in the first round, except for the 12 of the French Quo Vadis. One was eliminated, the others ranged from 20½ to 36½. It was obvious that the regular two-o'clock storm had caused the going to deteriorate even further. The combinations, already big enough, were now very formidable indeed.

Too formidable for little Stroller? one asked oneself anxiously.

In seconds we had the answer. Twice Stroller stopped in the middle of the treble. The second time he slid into the parallels and fell, one of the poles hitting Marion in the face. She was dazed; worse, she was shocked when she realised that Stroller could not rise. In fact, it was only because he was lying on his rein. By the time he was up the confused Marion assumed that she was eliminated. She remounted and rode slowly towards the exit. Suddenly Harvey Smith was seen rushing towards her, shouting at her to carry on. She came to herself, picked up Stroller and set off again for the treble, which somehow she got through – only for the bell to ring before she reached the next fence because by now she had exceeded the time limit. There were many who said that the bell had never been rung when the fence was knocked down as she refused, needing to be rebuilt before she could have a further attempt, but our old friend from Rome, Bruno Bruni, President of the Jury in Mexico, insisted that Marion had never held up her hand to show that she was ready to start again and that was why he had not stopped the clock. It has always been a confusing rule though attempts have been made to simplify it. My own opinion is that Stroller, only 14 hands 2 inches, had frightened himself at the very big combination which no horse cleared in the individual competition. His courage took him over the combinations in the first round of the team event, though he had faulted at both, but in the more difficult conditions of the afternoon, and doubtless feeling the abscess in his mouth, he just decided that enough was enough.

It goes without saying that there was the usual mix-up as to whether the whole team was now disqualified or whether our other riders could jump, with Stroller being given a score equal to the worst score in the round, plus 20. The Irish assumed the former, neither of the other Irish horses coming in after Barrymore's elimination. Harvey, I understand, thought differently, persuading our team manager to let him jump; which he did, for 26½ faults, though I am sure that he would have done better had that gold medal still been in sight – like everyone else connected with Britain he was shattered by Marion's experience. The ever-reliable, immensely experienced, David Broome had 12 faults, finishing up with the second best score of the day.

The scores tell their own story. Canada won the gold with a total of 102.75, the highest score ever recorded for the winning team in Olympic jumping; France won the silver with 110.50; Germany beat the USA for the bronze by $\frac{1}{4}$ fault, 117.25 to 117.50.

There is no doubt that the Mexico course, considering the conditions, was too big; big enough to spoil good, courageous horses. No Olympic course since Mexico has been so demanding. Since Mexico, too, the rules have changed so that, as in a Nations Cup, each team consists of four horses and riders, with the best three to count. Both in Rome and in Mexico it might well have been a different story had there been a fourth rider, allowing us to drop our riders who were eliminated. But, of course, it was the same for every nation. Nevertheless, certainly in retrospect, the Mexico Olympics was one of the most enjoyable experiences of my BBC days. Munich, four years later, was an experience, too: but of a very different kind.

Chapter 4

Triumph and Tragedy

Munich 1972
As so often seemed to happen, the Munich Olympic Games coincided with the Pendley Shakespeare Festival, which used to be the busiest fortnight of the year for me. I was directing two plays and responsible for the overall organisation for the Festival; and by 1972 it was attracting audiences in excess of 10,000. In addition, cubhunting usually started during the Festival; as Master of my local Hunt, the Whaddon Chase, I liked to be out whenever hounds were out, which in September was three or four mornings each week, starting at 7.00 a.m. At the end of the Festival, therefore, I expected to be tired, but in 1972 in addition to being tired I felt generally out of sorts. I was also depressed, partly due to the fact that for the first time since the Festival started in 1949 I was having to leave before the end. I had produced the first play, *Love's Labour's Lost*, which had been highly successful, but had been hard work, because, owing to the demand for tickets, we had had to start one day earlier, which allowed me only five full days' rehearsal: barely enough, with a cast, as it happened, less experienced than usual. It was all worth it, of course – if only for the hauntingly beautiful effect achieved by the horse-drawn carriage with the Princess of France and her ladies disappearing up the glade, its little lights twinkling, at the end of the play. The second play, produced by my old friend and Pendley veteran, Ronnie Evers, despite a more experienced cast, had had problems which needed much tact and patience before it finally enjoyed a successful first performance.

I had a difficult flight to Munich, culminating in the loss of my suitcase. I had not been informed that the luggage of BBC personnel had preferential treatment, finishing up in a special bay. When eventually I arrived at the Hotel Atlantico, on the very outskirts of Munich, it was entirely deserted except for the football commentator, Brian Butler, who kindly showed me the ropes and had a drink with me. My room was not inspiring, facing the back. Nor was the bed very comfortable; as I soon discovered, having decided to lie down for an hour, with nothing to do – no shops were within walking distance – and feeling far from well. Fortunately I did not have long to feel sorry for myself, as I was soon fully involved in the three-day event, which took place at Poing, about thirty miles north-east of Munich. I had never been particularly fond of Germany or the German race, but it was immediately apparent that everyone was out to be as helpful as possible. Even at the dressage everyone seemed relaxed and happy; usually one is expected to assume a hushed reverence more associated with a cathedral. At Poing I was soon among friends. One of the jury was my old friend Bruno Bruni; another was Senor Mangilli whom I had also met in Rome. Dr Specht, the general manager at the Reim headquarters, I had recently entertained at the British Equestrian Centre at Stoneleigh where I had organised an international instructors' conference. One of the Italian horses – British-bred Woodland, by Woodcut – was owned by Marie Sola Campello, who had been so hospitable in Rome. Hans Brinckmann, the most eminent course builder in the world had frequently been at international shows which I had attended. Then there were all my friends from the 'media' and, of course, many riders from different countries with whom I had become friendly. Finally there was the British contingent. Everyone seemed determined to make it an outstandingly happy occasion, to erase, perhaps, the pre-war reputation of Munich with its beer cellars, putschs and dictatorial oratory. Certainly at the end of the dressage the British supporters had reason to be happy, the British team having done exceptionally well with Mark Phillips on Great Ovation right at the top with a score of 36.33, Richard Meade on Lauriston being less than three marks behind him.

Despite the earliness of the start it was hot when we reached the cross-country course on the Friday morning. Once again there was no proper television, which, in Germany, disappointed me. A few cameras, dotted about the course, filmed the event; the film was then edited into a programme with dubbed commentary to be transmitted later in the evening. The loudspeaker system, too, was totally inadequate, carrying only a hundred yards or so beyond the score-board. This meant that one had frequently to make one's way back to the score-board to check results, having first attempted to see a particular rider over a particular jump. The miles that I must have covered that day! I remember being justifiably envious as, perspiring and exhausted, I hurried back from the complex of fences 17, 18 and 19, seeing one of the most beautiful girls I had ever seen on the arm of an enormously stout, beer-swilling Bavarian in traditional costume bursting at every seam. Obviously she adored him; equally obviously they had all the time in the world to enjoy their day out; and why not? But what has he got –? I thought, as I hurried back to see Mary Gordon-Watson finish on Cornishman V. I had seen them survive miraculously at 17, 18 and 19: a complex consisting of a steep bank, a fence at the bottom on to a road, a very big fence out of the road on to a bank, then sharp right-handed down a track to a huge spread. Breathless, I arrived just in time to see her over the last fence.

The score-board showed that Mark Phillips had had two falls which had knocked him right back, but Cornish Gold, ridden by Bridget Parker, despite a refusal at a seemingly innocuous double bank, had had a wonderful round to finish with 17.3 bonus points. (New scoring which puts the onus on speed, with a very tight allowance for the cross-country phase, has since been introduced. In 1972 one could earn bonus points by 'beating' the time allowance.) Mary Gordon-Watson, who also stopped at the double bank – apparently there was an awkward stride at the top – had done even better, for a bonus of 30.27.

Everything now depended on the last rider from each team. Germany obviously was the main threat to Britain, but when I recorded an interview with Mary she seemed confident that Richard Meade had nothing to fear. 'It's a marvellous course', she said, but, as I reminded her, it was easier to say that when she had just successfully completed it. Her confidence, however, was quickly given a boost when the German ace,

Horst Karsten, withdrew after a horrific fall at some rails on his normally reliable Sioux; and then Michael Plumb, from America, on Free and Easy had a fall. The tension during Richard Meade's round on Lauriston, owned and bred by Derek Allhusen, team gold and individual silver medallist in Mexico – surely a good omen – was almost unbearable. One attempted to be in about three places at once; why the BBC had not been provided with a Land Rover I cannot remember, but one would certainly have been welcome.

Managing, again, to reach the finish just as Richard Meade approached the last two fences – zig-zag rails and a low rail in front of a ditch, delightfully described on the course plan as *scheezaun* and *tripplebarre von graben* – we had worked out that if Richard reached the finish in fifteen minutes or less then Britain must be in the lead. When, according to my stop-watch, he finished in the fastest time of the day it was obvious that he must have gone clear. When I interviewed him as soon as he had dismounted I was more out of breath than he was. By our calculation at the end of the cross-country the British team were so far ahead that they could afford seven fences down in the show jumping next day and still win; though, as Richard said in the interview, it is easy enough to lose your way – memories of poor Pavel Deev, in Mexico, who was *not* at Munich – or collect a cricket score – memories of his own round on Barbery in Tokyo. In the individual he could afford just one fence down, as the Italian Alessandro Argenton on Marie Sola's horse, Woodland, was breathing down his neck. I was by no means sanguine myself, having seen so many upturns of fortune, though I was assured that I sounded buoyant in the transmission that night. And all indeed went well. At Reim, where the jumping took place, Richard's clear round ensured his individual gold. Mary Gordon-Watson and Mark Phillips also went clear, while Bridget Parker had just one fence down to finish tenth. Britain had some 80 points in hand over the USA and more than 100 over West Germany.

Once again my voice was stifled with emotion as first the National Anthem was played for the individual, then for the team. It was a moment of glorious triumph. Exhausted as I was I felt too elated to sleep, but perversely found my mind filled, not only with the excitements at Reim, but equally with the end of the Festival back at Pendley which, for the first time, I was missing: the midnight matinée with that little coach disappearing up the glade, a thousand contented people wandering down the lawns to their cars – or the bar where some of the players would join them. Was it really only four days since I had left them? It seemed a month. I found myself wondering, too, how the cubhunting had gone at Christmas Gorse; always one of my favourite fixtures in early September.

The following day, the Sunday, we had the individual jumping out at Reim which raised our spirits even more. At the end of the first round there were only three clears: Jim Day for Canada, Graziano Mancinelli for Italy and Ann Moore for Britain. There were about eight with 4 faults, David Broome and Mike Saywell each having 8. The second round, for which only the best twenty qualified, was a different matter. Over the bigger course there were bigger scores. David Broome had 12, Mike Saywell 16, Fritz Ligges and Gerd Wiltfang, for Germany, had 12 and 28 respectively, Kathy Kusner, USA, had 16, Hartwig Steenken had only 4 to add to his first round 4; but $\frac{3}{4}$ of a time fault denied him the jump-off, as did just $\frac{1}{4}$ time fault added to Jim Day's second round 8. There were no clears, but Neil Shapiro, from the USA, who had had 4 faults in the first round had another 4, for a total of 8; both Mancinelli and Ann Moore, clear in the first round, had 8; so the three had to jump-off for the gold. Neil Shapiro, going first on Sloopy, had two fences down in a slow time (the horse was jumping in a bandage, having badly cut its leg schooling over water earlier in the week. Mancinelli, riding the Irish-bred Ambassador like a man possessed, was clear in 48 seconds, bringing off an incredible S-turn into the treble. Ann Moore, knowing that she could not get away with such a turn on Psalm, tried to save time cutting into the second fence, right in the corner, a 5 ft 5 in upright; but she came in at too much of an angle and Psalm stopped. Three faults. Nevertheless, even with the stop, she finished only just over 8 seconds slower than Mancinelli. Watching it later on television I estimated that her stop cost her 10 seconds. How near she had gone to a gold – and what a wonderful double for our eventers and show jumpers that would have been!

All the same there was more than enough to celebrate with

the silver; and celebrate we did the next night at a dinner party organised by Paul Schockemohle, in a smart restaurant in the centre of Munich. To my delight I found myself sitting next to Ann Moore. As I might have guessed, sitting the other side of Ann was David Broome, for they were having a big affair at the time; and as I might have guessed, too, she had not very much time for me – except when she was actually eating she had her head on the tender lap of David! On my other side was a German rider who did not speak English. Finding myself playing gooseberry once again, however, did not in any way prevent my sharing the British contingent's near-euphoria, which was heightened by the immensely happy impression that we had all formed of the city and the people. This had surprised me, but it was a fact that nothing seemed too much trouble for our hosts. They were determined that we were to enjoy ourselves. Officialdom and officiousness were kept to a minimum; security was never obtrusive.

This lack of security was emphasised by an amusing incident at the end of the three-day event jumping at Reim. Having just recorded an introduction to the programme, which was to go out later, in the BBC's scanner outside the stadium, I jumped down the steps only to collide with Prince Philip who was walking past, completely unattended and apparently unrecognised. As I stood talking to him two small German boys rushed up, brandishing their autograph books. Prince Philip waved them away, muttering in German something obviously to the effect that he did not sign autographs. But pushing past him they accosted me with their books. To young Germans Prince Philip was probably quite unknown, but to any young boy anyone in any way connected with television must be a celebrity and, therefore, worth asking for an autograph. Naturally I was somewhat embarrassed, but Prince Philip, even if a little surprised, did not seem in the least put out as he wandered off, still unattended, mixing with the crowds pouring from the stadium.

The next two days were free: the first day was taken up with celebrating, parties and receptions, but on the Monday, my tiredness caught up with me as the excitement of the British successes abated, and so I spent the whole day in my room resting and reading – *The Boston Strangler*, I remember! –

frustrated at being unable to get through to England on my
room telephone. Alone at dinner in the hotel I noticed two
charming young American girls, sitting at a nearby table
looking rather shy and lost. I should have liked to talk to them,
as if ever they caught my eye they smiled pleasantly, giving
the impression that they would like to be sociable, but I was
determined to go to bed early, as I and my BBC colleague,
Peter Marsh, had to leave the hotel at 6.00 a.m. to go to
Nymphenburg Palace, the summer residence of the old rulers
of Bavaria, where the Grand Prix Dressage was being held.

Punctually at six o'clock I met Peter Marsh in the foyer of
our hotel, boarded our car, driven as usual by a student, and
set off for Nymphenburg. Our driver had his radio on; it
appeared to be the news and he was listening intently. Neither
Peter nor I spoke German, but it was quite obvious that our
young driver was listening to something very dramatic. After
a few minutes we gathered, from a series of gestures and
pidgin English, that whatever it was that was happening was
connected with the Olympic village. Again and again our
driver uttered exclamations of horror, even from time to time
throwing up his hands. Peter acted quickly and ordered the
driver to take us back to the hotel; but even after reaching the
hotel, when Peter had leapt out and dashed up to the room of
Bryan Cowgill, BBC's Head of Sport, I could not really
believe the implication of the driver's mime – handling a gun,
accompanied by a rat-a-tat-tat, as in a childish game. In less
than five minutes Peter Marsh had reappeared with Bryan
Cowgill, who told our driver to take us to the studios. These
were within a hundred yards or so of the village. While Bryan
Cowgill was organising the immediate deployment of
cameras I found myself watching, as if in some bizarre
nightmare, masked gunmen prowling up and down the
balconies of the village with sawn-off shotguns. Could I ever,
even in my wildest flights of imagination, have envisaged
myself looking at murderers and terrorists in action at, of all
places, the Olympic Games? One could only stand there,
totally incredulous. Within a few minutes we had, rightly,
been instructed to carry on to Nymphenburg. There was
nothing useful that we could do at the studios or at the village.
(Raymond Brooks-Ward was more fortunate(?): he was

immediately conscripted as a commentator for sound radio.)

By now it was about 7.00 a.m. and the most glorious early autumn morning. Nymphenburg was of breathtaking beauty, with its palace consisting of a central building flanked by two smaller buildings, its ornamental gardens and its long 'canal' – a mile long lake, with other more natural lakes either side, leading to a waterfall. The dressage arena was in front of the house at the head of the canal. On such a morning the whole lay-out was almost exquisitely unreal: too beautiful to be believed. There was not a cloud in the sky, only a murmur of water and the singing of the birds in the great trees that were the dominating feature in this paradise: all in such contrast to the Olympic village on Lerchenaur Strasse. I was reminded of the outbreak of the Second World War: 3 September, 1939, just thirty-three years ago and two days earlier. Then, too, it was a glorious autumn morning. I was at Hawtreys School, at Westgate-on-Sea. Having heard Chamberlain at 11.00 a.m. announce that we were at war I was strolling down Harold Avenue between the two parts of the school with a friend when the sirens went off. Thanet being about as near to Germany as anywhere in Britain, bombs at any minute might have been falling out of that cloudless sky, shattering the peace and the beauty of the morning. It was, of course, a false alarm and we continued our stroll. But it was no false alarm at Munich. The village was now in a state of seige.

The Grand Prix de Dressage was due to start at 8.00 a.m. with what seemed an appropriately named horse, Sod, ridden by Hermann Duer from Switzerland. We were not due to record until Jennie Loriston-Clarke did her test on Kadett at about 9.15 a.m., but we went immediately to our 'cubicle' where Peter at once established contact with the studio. The situation at the village appeared to be very 'fluid', a euphemism for nobody having a clue as to exactly what was happening.

At about 10.30 a.m., while we were waiting for Christine Stueckelberger on Granat – my first sight of this great horse which was to win gold medals in the World and European Championships and at the Montreal Olympics – the curtain across the door of our cubicle was suddenly drawn aside and in walked none other than Edward Heath, then Prime Minister.

Nobody seemed able to tell him where the VIP seats were, he explained. He saw BBC on the door of our cubicle so he thought that we would not mind if he joined us, but we were not to allow him to disturb us. He would, all the same, like to know if there was any news from the village. Peter immediately contacted the studio and was able to give the Prime Minister the latest news which was, apparently, still 'fluid'. Quite an experience to feel that one is keeping the Prime Minister informed at a time of crisis!

I asked Mr Heath if he had ever watched dressage before.

'Once', he replied, 'but I will not pretend that it is my favourite sport.' In fact, he could not wait, he said, to get out to Kiel to the sailing; but first he had to attend a lunch for all the British medallists. I told him that there were two particularly charming young ladies whose company he would enjoy, Mary Gordon-Watson and Ann Moore. At a reception that evening both Mary and Ann told me that they had met Edward Heath, how friendly he had been and how much he seemed to know about their performances!

Late in the afternoon we filmed Lorna Johnstone's test on El Farruco, being delighted that she just managed to make the reprise, or barrage, in 12th place with a score of 1576, compared with the German Liselott Linsenhoff's 1763 on Piaff and the Russian Elena Petuschkova's 1747 on Pepel. I personally greatly preferred the fluent Pepel to the heavy accuracy of Piaff, but again the variations in the marks of the different judges seemed to make nonsense of the judging. There was, for instance, with Pepel, over 40 marks' difference between two judges. In the team event Britain was 10th out of 10; but no one could blame the judges for that. In the final, however, two judges differed by over 40 marks on Lorna Johnstone's test and, for the first and only time that I have ever heard at top-class dressage, there was prolonged boo-ing. Mrs Johnstone finally finished 12th, but her score of 1036 compared with the winner Piaff's 1229 was in no way a disgrace. Indeed, only one British rider has achieved more in the Olympics: Christopher Bartle, who finished 6th in Los Angeles in 1984.

We called in at the studio on the way back to our hotel. Not surprisingly in that more or less organised chaos we felt somewhat *de trop*. There was no doubt that the situation had become increasingly ugly, with nobody seeming to know what was going to happen next, or how best to handle the situation. Many people thought that the Games should be abandoned. Fortunately common sense prevailed, though my own opinion was that it might have been sensible to discontinue anthems and flag-raising especially after the even more serious carnage at the airport. Had such a decision been taken it is just possible that the emphasis on nationalism might have disappeared for ever, to the inevitable benefit of the Olympic movement which should only be concerned with competition between individuals, not with competition between nations. When I arrived back at my hotel I felt almost physically sick. That in the space of minutes something that had been so joyous could be transformed into something so horrifically evil was a tragedy. The Games, I was convinced, could never recover; any more than could our spirits which less than twenty-four hours earlier had been so buoyant.

Again I failed to get through to my home on the telephone. Thinking that it might be a problem with the country code I rang a friend in London and asked her if she would kindly telephone my wife, Jennifer, and ask her to ring me immediately. But there was no call and before very long I found myself uncharacteristically wallowing in depression – by nature I am optimistic and resilient – but I had not felt well since my arrival in Munich. Cancellation of the next day's programme in order to hold a memorial service in the stadium – which only ten days earlier had been the scene of the brilliant, confident Opening Ceremony – underlined the incredible drama in which we were all now involved: it also meant that the Olympics were extended by one day – so it would be one day longer before I got home. I knew that I must pull myself together. It was no good lying on my bed moping.

The previous evening as the American girls left the dining-room I had said hello to them. Immediately the elder one became very voluble, obviously nervous as well as shy. She knew, of course, who I was, she told me, and had actually read some of my books; it was exciting to meet me personally; she had always wanted to, but of course never thought that she would. There had been a mix-up over their bookings so they had found themselves in this hotel on the outskirts of the city with no transport and no 'subway' anywhere near. They had only twice managed to get to Olympic events, thanks to the kindness of strangers, though they had tickets for every day, but it was wonderful being at the Olympics, and staying at the same hotel as so many celebrities; there'd be so much to tell them back home in Kentucky. They'd never believe it. Gradually she relaxed, allowing her sister to tell me a little more about themselves. I took the opportunity to introduce them to Bill Steinkraus, David Broome, David Coleman, Douglas Bunn and a few others as they passed our table on their way out. Finally they thanked me very prettily – it had been just marvellous to talk to me, and so helpful – and went to their room.

Now, on impulse, remembering their room number, which they had mentioned at some time during our conversation, I dialled it. The elder one – her name was Jean – answered it immediately, almost as if she had been awaiting the call – as I had been awaiting mine from home. I asked if they would like to have dinner with me. There was a moment's silence. I thought I could hear whispering. Then she said that it really was terribly unfortunate, absolutely maddening, but someone in the same party that had come over from America was taking them out to dinner. Obviously the younger sister had insisted that she could not get out of it, however much she wanted to. Tomorrow then? I suggested. Oh no, they had to go home tomorrow, they had to stick to their original flight although the Games had been extended. Oh well, never mind; disappointed, I was about to put down my receiver, but no, please, we must meet; she sounded almost desperate. She wanted very much to talk to me. What about a drink then before they went out? Tonight? Oh, yes, that would be lovely. What time? Six o'clock in the bar by the foyer? Fine.

She was on her own when she met me in the attractive little hotel bar. She was probably twenty-one or twenty-two, nicely dressed, pretty in an American way, but tense, though when she started talking she now sounded surprisingly relaxed. The recent death of her mother had obviously affected her profoundly. She had wanted to go to college, but felt guilty at leaving her father; she wanted to write, but nobody took her seriously. She talked almost without ceasing in a

simple, honest, straightforward manner. I listened, occasionally making a sympathetic comment. After half an hour or so
her sister joined us. Conversation then became general: the
Olympics, my life in England, our respective interests. Suddenly over the intercom there was a call in German, culminating in 'Fraulein Murphy'. It was their host. They rose to go.
Quite naturally, as though I were a favourite uncle, Jean
reached up and kissed me affectionately; her sister followed
suit, then as Jean moved away, whispered to me, 'I don't
know what you've done to Jean. It's marvellous: thank you so
much.'

That was all. I never saw them again. A curious interlude in
my Munich Olympics; not entirely irrelevant as it had a
certain significance for me in that it not only showed me that
other people could be unhappy too, but that I was capable in a
small way of helping them, if only by being there at the right
moment. I felt a quite different person when I went in to
dinner, even inviting myself to someone else's table, rather
than eating on my own, with my book, as had been my wont.

For a year or so Jean Murphy wrote me lengthy letters from
Kentucky telling me of her triumphs and disasters, her father's
remarriage and finally her own marriage. If I had in a humble
way been able to help her at a rather critical moment in her life,
there is no doubt that our brief encounter at the Hotel
Atlantico had been a real, if somewhat unconventional, benefit to me.

The final event, the team show jumping, immediately
before the Closing Ceremony, contained incidents of such
high drama that for a few hours one was able to forget the
horrors of the preceding week. The stadium was shrouded in
something akin to a sea mist, or fret, when we arrived at 7.00
a.m. It was bitterly cold; only Anders Goersan, the Swedish
commentator, was protected from the cold as, still holding
army rank, he was entitled to an army blanket. The rest of us
in our eeries high up in the stand almost froze to death. In the
opinion of most experts the contest lay between West Germany, the United States, Italy and Britain. The first round
suggested a nail-biting finish with the United States just $\frac{1}{4}$ fault
behind West Germany, while Britain and Spain were equal
less than two fences behind. Nothing went right for Italy in

the second round, with an appalling performance by the individual gold medallist Mancinelli and elimination for Piero d'Inzeo. Then came the dramatic climax. Each German rider had had 4 faults to give them a total of 32 for the two rounds. For America Shapiro went clear, Chapot had a good 8, Kathy Kusner 12. This meant that if Steinkraus went clear with Main Spring America would win; but one fence down and they would lose to Germany by the ½ time fault that Shapiro had picked up in the first round. As was usually the case with the de Nemethy-Freined Americans Steinkraus, who had ridden an effortless clear in the first round, looked enviably confident as he set off over Brinckmann's big course, Main Spring jumping superbly. We were just beginning to think that it was all over bar the shouting when at the water, which by my measurement barely reached the 16 ft it was alleged to be and which had caused very little trouble all day, Main Spring completely failed to take off, trailing his hind legs through the fence and belly-flopping into the water. Somehow Steinkraus stayed on board, but it was 4 faults. Germany had won by ½ a fault.

I can hear to this day the reaction of that great 80,000 crowd; but it is almost impossible to describe. A yell of disbelief, a gasp of horror from the sizeable American contingent, a roar of delight, impossible to suppress, from the West German audience, all welded into a kind of staccato shriek, which expanded into an excited murmur, finally to be drowned by the universal roar of applause as Steinkraus completed the course.

It was bitterly disappointing for America, of course, but Britain seemed poised to take the bronze. In the second round Harvey Smith got Summertime round with just 4 faults, Mike Saywell had two fences down on Hideaway, Ann Moore on Psalm – almost uncannily emulating Marion Mould in Mexico – having won the silver in the individual now stopped twice, as had Stroller, in the treble. Only by the most determined riding did she get Psalm through at the third attempt, and fortunately, unlike Marion, did not run out of time. Not that it would have been a major disaster for Britain had she been eliminated, as it was in Mexico, for now, in the Grand Prix Team event, each nation fielded four with the best three to count. And last to jump for Britain was David Broome on Manhattan, not the greatest horse that he had ever ridden, but he was one of only half a dozen that had had just 4 faults in the first round. He now had four fences in hand. His bad start soon had our hearts in our mouths. He had down the second fence – straightforward upright rails at 5 ft 2 in – and the first part of the fourth, the double – rustic poles at 5 ft 1½ in. He could still have two fences down and clinch the bronze, but there was the fearsome treble that had caught out so many during the day. To our intense relief he sailed through it magnificently. Only the last two fences, a double oxer, 5 ft 1 in high, 6 ft 7 in wide, and an upright at 5 ft 2 in – but crash went the oxer! Still he had that one fence in hand – surely he must clear the last, practically every horse in the competition had done so, but no – Manhattan just did not rise high enough. Indeed, he seemed to have given David very little throughout the whole round, except at the treble.

Sixteen faults. The British contingent, including the commentator, watched in stunned silence as muted applause followed David from the great stadium. We had been beaten for the bronze by Italy, by just three points. We had scarcely expected to beat Germany on their own ground, but having won five of the eight Nations Cups in which we had competed that season, coming second in two others and third in another, we felt confident that we would be amongst the medals, as, seemingly, did everyone else. It was a sad anti-climax, though a tremendously dramatic finale to the event, first with Steinkraus going for the gold, then with Broome going for the bronze. Disappointment must have shown in my voice, commentating, even frustration, for at the Horse of the Year Show a few weeks later I was berated by David Broome's mother for blaming him for our losing the bronze medal. Far from being offended I was delighted that after all David's triumphs, success and failure still meant so much to him and to his family. Nevertheless, after so much it was frustrating to end on an unhappy note, though it was not, I am sure, sour grapes that found me so disenchanted with the Closing Ceremony, spoiled as it was – for me – with undisciplined junketings and rowdiness, singing and dancing and horseplay through the speeches and various ceremonies. Such lack of dignity seemed sadly out of harmony with the mood that had prevailed since the tragic event six days earlier. If only they had been content to finish with the brilliant Quadrille presented by the twelve leading German dressage riders, including Dr Klimke, Harry Boldt, Liselotte Linsenhoff, Joseph Neckermann, Willi Schultheis and Inge Theodorescue; it can only be described as something out of this world, the like of which will never be seen again.

It did not surprise me that I arrived home late the next evening feeling tired and depressed, nor that Jennifer appeared shocked at my appearance. Yet although it explained much, I was not at all prepared to learn a few weeks later that I had cancer.

Aachen

It seemed that circumstances were determined to leave me with an unhappy recollection of Munich. Indeed, I do not, on the whole, have happy memories of any of my visits to Germany. My first was in 1957 when the BBC sent me to some vast estate where once a year wild ponies were rounded up and culled. The method of doing this was for wardens to drive a herd of ponies towards the village where the youths would be waiting to catch them – by tackling them, as if they were playing rugger, when they galloped past. From every point of view it was appalling television. The cameras seldom seemed to be pointed in the right direction for the 'incidents'– many of which were horrific as two or three youths fought with a pony before wrestling it to the ground, sitting on its head until someone else came up and roped it. From the British viewers' point of view, moreover, it made very unattractive viewing, as viewers left me in no doubt. In addition, the German television producer spoke no English, nor did his assistant, so it was quite impossible for me to understand the 'niceties' or 'techniques' of the sport; I could only describe what I saw, which I did not like.

My next visit to Germany was to Aachen in 1961 for the European Show Jumping Championships. Again I was alone, just flying out in time for the finale, which consisted of the four leading riders riding each other's horses. Most unfortunately the person at Lime Grove in charge of the arrangements had

mistakenly interpreted 14.00 hours as 4.00 p.m.! Conse-
quently, by the time the BBC came on the air the whole event
was over. As soon as I had arrived, at about 2.00 p.m., I
managed to contact the BBC and explain, but their reaction
was simply to insist that I have the finale delayed, which was
not simple at all; in fact, with no Bruno Bruni, it was
impossible. It was, of course, before the days of video which
enables a producer to record and edit a programme, transmitting it later. The result was that viewers at home missed an
extremely exciting finale with Steinkraus on Ksar d'Esprit,
Piero d'Inzeo on Pioneer, Hans Winkler on Romanus and
David Broome on Sunsalve. The rules were – as in those days
for a World Championship, but not often used today – that the
leading four should all ride each other's horses. This
sometimes led to a certain amount of gamesmanship, a rider
tending to choose the horse of his top string that was the most
difficult to ride. Sunsalve was David Broome's outstanding
horse at that time and he would have chosen it anyway, but it
was a very difficult horse for anyone to ride, let alone someone
who had never ridden it before. Each rider is allowed only a
two minutes 'warm-up' before entering the ring on his rival's
horse. D'Inzeo's Pioneer cannot have been an easy ride for a
newcomer either, while to get the best out of Ksar d'Esprit or
Romanus obviously one had to ride them in the American and
German style respectively, and the two styles are very dissimilar. In the last of the four rounds, Steinkraus was riding
Sunsalve, this notoriously strong and difficult horse, so unlike
an American-trained horse. He could still win, beating David
himself, but he had to go clear to do so. All went well until the
water where Sunsalve gave him a crashing fall, standing off a
full two strides before the take-off. This left David, who had
achieved masterly rounds on each of the three horses that were
strange to him, as the outright winner, stamping him, then
just twenty, as a champion if ever there was one. I wonder
sometimes if Steinkraus recalled that calamity as he
approached the water on Main Spring at Munich in the
Olympic Games eleven years later.

I was staying at a little hotel just off the main square, not
much more than a boarding house, but comfortable with good
food. I had to catch a train at 7.00 a.m. in order to reach

Dusseldorf in time for my plane. I arranged for a taxi to pick
me up at 6.00 a.m., but it never turned up. There was no
member of the staff, which for the most part just consisted of
the proprietor and his family, awake at that hour; the streets
were as asleep as they are in any city at 6.00 a.m. on a Sunday
morning. I had no idea where the station was, or how far from
the hotel. I was getting desperate, wandering off in the
direction of the square when, miraculously, I spied a taxi
passing across the top of the square. Using all the considerable
voice at my command I shouted. To my relief he heard me,
and I caught my train.

It was experience with trains that made my next visit to
Germany, in 1965, somewhat memorable. My BBC colleague on that occasion was Ian Smith. He flew straight out
from the Men's Singles Finals at Wimbledon where the
temperature had been in the nineties. He arrived exhausted,
had a large beer and went immediately to bed, as we had an
early start. This time our taxi picked us up and we caught our
train, but we had hardly started our journey before Ian started
an appalling nose-bleed. Blood flowed as from a fountain. We
tried everything to stem it, but all to no avail. Eventually
when the train stopped at a station I dashed to a buffet and
filled a glass with ice, terrified that the train would leave
without me. To our relief it worked. We had no more trouble,
but poor Ian was very distressed at the state of his clothes,
including a new lightweight suit. When we reached Aachen
station that evening, having seen Hermann Schridde win the
European Championship with Alwin Schockemohle third, to
the delight of the huge German audience, we had no idea of the
time of our train, and nor apparently had anyone else. First we
were told to go to one platform, then we were told that it was
another platform, then another, and so on. It was like a comic
film with us rushing from one platform to another, boarding
as the whistle blew, only to discover that it was the wrong
train and leaping off just in time. Finally we struggled on to a
train as it was actually pulling out of the station. From a fellow
passenger we understood that it was the trans-continental
express, but did it stop at Dusseldorf? He did not know. It
seemed unlikely. At that moment I saw a large stewardess
walking down the corridor carrying about eight green cham-

berpots in each hand, like fistfuls of cauliflowers. I hurried after her. Dusseldorf, I asked; Dusseldorf? She stopped and looked at me as if such a question was the last thing she could be expected to answer. For a moment I thought that she was going to crown me with the chamberpots, but she stood there, thought for a moment and then said, in English, 'Sometimes'. Fortunately this turned out to be one of the times that it did.

My last visit to Aachen was in 1978 when I went over for the World Championships, in which Gerd Wiltfang ultimately beat Eddie Macken by $\frac{1}{4}$ fault. I flew to Cologne and picked up a car which gave me more independence, but I had the greatest difficulty in finding my hotel, despite the fact that I had stayed there twice before. Having driven up and down streets and round and round the square I finally found a parking space and decided that I must set out on foot to find the hotel. There was a man just getting into the next car. I started hesitantly in pidgin English to ask if he knew my hotel, or even the street. It turned out, fortunately, that he was an Englishman whose office was in the same street as the hotel. I had two free days between our transmissions which gave me the opportunity to explore the very impressive city centre. First, of course, there was the magnificent Gothic Cathedral founded by Charlemagne with the octagonal cupola and its renowned treasures including the Lothar Cross. The Rathaus, or City Hall, built in the fourteenth century, was also extremely impressive, but almost the most enjoyable for me was the eighteenth-century house maintained exactly, to the very last detail, as it was 250 years ago. Altogether a happy two or three days, comparable to those first few days of the Munich Games when, before the disaster, everything had been so relaxed and carefree.

Inevitably, the tragedy of Munich left an unpalatable legacy to the Olympics, from which they were going to find it difficult wholly to recover.

Chapter 5

Last Gasp from the Olympics

Montreal 1976

The presence of Princess Anne in the British three-day event team obviously heightened the interest in the equestrian events in the Montreal Olympics, both with the general public and with the press, but particularly, of course, with the horse world. As a result there seemed more people than ever at Bromont, where the equestrian events were being held. Bromont, which in some publications had been accorded the status of city was, in fact, a small town in the Eastern Townships, founded only in 1964, about fifty miles from Montreal, with a population of 2000. The invasion of 70,000 spectators put a considerable strain on the town and this was not helped by the strict security arrangements, which were not always well administered. For instance, there was a private road from the centre of Bromont down to the actual site of the events, but this was available only to officials. Instead of police being stationed at the top of the road where one turned off the main street they were about 100 yards down the track, which meant that every single vehicle, other than those with official badges, had to be turned back. The traffic chaos can be imagined. Fortunately being with the BBC I had an official's pass.

The first day of the three-day event dressage took place on Thursday 22 July. It was a beautiful day with the spectacular Brome mountains to the north – 'a child of nature endowed with a beautiful profile' – making a magnificent backdrop. Princess Anne was the first to ride for Britain, on Goodwill, the horse that the Queen had bought for her from Alison Dawes. Goodwill, which had been a successful Grade A show jumper, was a big 16.2 hh by Evening Trial; he was now eleven years old. The start of his test was excellent, so much so that when he strode across the arena on the diagonal in a tremendous extended trot the large audience broke into applause, after which he never really settled; in fact, at the end he was distinctly gassy, finishing up with a score of 91.25, compared with the West German Karl Schultz's 46.25. Richard Meade on the 17 hh, eight-year-old Jacob Jones, was very steady for a score of 73.75. On the second day Hugh Thomas on the ten-year-old Playamar, apart from an explosion in the middle of his test, did well enough for 85, while Lucinda Prior-Palmer, as she then was, on her brilliant Be Fair, by Fair and Square, now nearing the end of his career, had a good 62.91 to put her among the top ten. At the end of the dressage Britain was well pleased to be in third place. But it was, of course, the cross-country that would count.

On the Wednesday, a very pleasant summer's day, I had walked the course with the team and Bill Lithgow, their *chef d'equipe*. As always, it appeared to me to be a course that was plenty big enough, the worst fences, as I saw it, being the 'slalom', an appallingly difficult complex on the side of a hill in a wood, involving three extremely tight turns between the trees; a fence for some reason called Debbie's Dilemma, a very 'airy' obstacle, 4 ft 10 in rails on to a steep slope; and the water sequence, an upturned boat into a lake with a brush fence out on to a bank. Walking the course I meticulously took the measurement of every single one of the 33 fences, except Fence 19 which I heard Bill Lithgow describe as a pony-club fence – zig-zag poles over a little ditch. The riders were instructed to jump it on the extreme right as they would then save precious seconds in going on to Fence 20, imposing rails, 4 ft 5 in high over a stream, 6 ft 2 in wide. Fairly exhausted after our 4½ mile walk, we were happy to accept the invitation of Laurence and Jane Rook to an al fresco lunch at the little house that they had rented up in the woods. The whole team was there, all of them in excellent spirits, as was the team reserve Mark Phillips, who had walked the course with Princess Anne, discussing every fence and advising her. Many people had felt that it was a mistake to have left out Mark Phillips with his immense experience. He had two sound horses in the eight-year-old Favour and the nine-year-old Persian Holiday, which stood 17.2 hh, while it was common knowledge that two of the four

riders selected for the team had horses with doubts. But if
Mark was disappointed, as indeed, he must have been, he gave
no sign of it, only wishing to be as helpful as he could in giving
the team the benefit of all that he had learned since first he was
reserve in Mexico eight years earlier.

I was not at all surprised to hear the rain pouring down
during the night before the cross-country. Next morning it
rained all the way to Bromont where the course, with a good
deal of standing water, looked very different from when we
had walked it in the sunshine three days earlier. The good
going was now heavy, there were soft patches, and water was
running down the tracks through the wood. First to go was
Dennis Piggott for Australia. His 'provisional' score of 153.6
was not encouraging; nor did the next horse, Woodland,
owned by our old friend Marie Sola Campello and ridden by
Allesandro Argentin, do any better. Their 'provisional' score
was 172. But, of course, it was Britain's first rider whom we
were anxiously awaiting, Princess Anne on Goodwill. We had
heard that they were clear on the steeplechase course. By the
time that she had reached the start of the cross-country it had
stopped raining, but the going was more rather than less
treacherous. I had made my way to the second fence, as I
believed that this was the one that might cause the biggest
problem for Goodwill. A very steep slide, about 15 ft down,
led to solid rails standing at 3 ft 9 in with a dry ditch in front. If
a horse came down the bank too fast the likelihood was that it
would be unable to take off, crashing into the rails. It was
essential to approach it very slowly, take two steady steps
down the bank, then stand off well before the bottom. Could
Goodwill who, we knew, was very strong, especially so early
on in the course, manage this? He could and he did. It was a
copybook performance and brought a roar from the crowd
who had seen both the two previous riders crash into the rails.
Away went Princess Anne over the very imposing parallels,
4 ft high, 6 ft wide, at the top of the hill and on to the rails into
the wood where she was lost to sight.

Somehow I managed to get to a vantage point where I could
see her thread her way brilliantly through the slalom and on to
the Golfer's Staircase, which Goodwill appeared to take
effortlessly, before striding down the hill through the trees.

This was getting exciting. They seemed to be devouring the course with devastating confidence and skill, certainly faster than any previous competitor. I waited now for her to appear at the airy rails, Fence 16. Goodwill put in a huge jump, landing right down the bank, Princess Anne sitting back and letting the reins slip through her fingers. Fence 17, 'Fort Rousseau', was a palisade; Fence 18 an open 'V' of 4 ft rails in front of a stream. As Princess Anne approached the zig-zag, Fence 19, I started off for the water, fences 22 and 23, only watching her through the corner of my eye as I knew that this 'pony-club' fence would hold no terrors for Goodwill. As instructed she made for the right-hand corner. Unfortunately some vital information that had been sent back to the start had never reached her, or, more accurately, had just missed her.

It is the usual practice on these occasions for the *chef d'equipe* to arrange for 'supporters' to be present at every single fence on the course, either to give assistance if it is needed – catching a horse after a fall for instance – or to pass to headquarters important information. The 'supporter' at Fence 19, Mike Bullen, had appreciated as soon as he had seen the first few horses over the zig-zag that thanks to the heavy rain there was a dangerously boggy patch on the right-hand side of the fence, just where our riders had been told that they should take off. Immediately a 'runner' was despatched to the start to suggest that Bill Lithgow should warn Princess Anne and the other members of our team. To get to the start, nearly two miles away, one had to climb up through the wood to the top of the hill before descending to the beginning of the course. Not surprisingly, in the humid conditions, the 'runner' was out of breath and quite exhausted by the time that he had reached the slalom near the top. Seeing a boy with a bicycle he asked him if he knew his way to the start. On being assured that he did the 'runner' scribbled a message on a page from his programme, telling the boy to deliver it to a tall man with a thick white moustache and a panama hat – Bill Lithgow. Off the boy went on his bike, but half way down, it seems, the chain came off. Instead of free-wheeling down the rest of the way he decided to mend it. It only took a few moments, but those moments were crucial. As the boy delivered his precious message to Bill Lithgow Princess Anne was disappearing over the first fence.

It was a sensational fall at Fence 19, which I saw with horror
from a distance. Both Princess Anne and Goodwill lay there
motionless. Through my glasses I saw with relief Goodwill
rise and led away, but Princess Anne continued to lie there as
the minutes ticked by. Then to mine and everyone else's
enormous relief she was helped to her feet. It was all made
even more dramatic for the huge crowd spread all over the
course by the failure, at this particular moment, of the
loudspeaker system. For those unable to see that part of the
course in which Fence 19 was situated there had been no
information of any sort since Princess Anne had been reported
safely over Fence 17. Amongst those waiting anxiously were
the Queen and Prince Philip in their Land Rover. After some
six minutes, with great courage and against the advice of Mike
Bullen and others, Princess Anne remounted and rode on. She
was, in fact, so dazed that she set off in the wrong direction
having to be corrected by Mike Bullen. She was later to tell me
that she had no recollection whatever of the remainder of that
round, but the film shows her surviving a remarkable mistake
at the water complex. Goodwill, despite his shaking, completed the course, magnificently, cleverly twisting his way
through the rookery, hopping up Dunlavey's banks – giant
steps – sailing over the log pile and striding on to the straw
bales in a manger at the end. But, of course, there were some
164.8 time penalties to be added to her 60 penalties for a fall.
For British supporters and, I believe many others, it was a
sickening and disappointing result for Princess Anne. We
could only hope that our other riders would be more
fortunate. At least they knew that they must avoid the right-
hand side of Fence 19. Playamar had a fall and time faults for a
score of 156, but both Richard Meade and Lucinda Green were
in the fifties, which was excellent as, thanks to the ridiculously
tightly measured course, every single competitor had time
faults. In fact, the lowest score of all was that of America's
Edmund (Tad) Coffin who, despite a clear round, could only
finish with 44 penalty points.

Be Fair's round at the end was one of the usual brilliance that
over the years we had come to expect, so that, until the bad
news reached us at the end of the day, we calculated that with
Richard Meade's good score and, compared with most, the

fair score of Hugh Thomas Britain as a team was lying in
second place, Princess Anne's score, of course, being the one
that had been discarded. America was leading us by 33 points,
less than four fences down for the whole team in the show
jumping. West Germany was a similar distance behind
Britain. But, of course, the bad news which meant inevitably
that our team was eliminated, was to the effect that Be Fair had
sprung an Achilles tendon at one of the last two fences, and
Playamar had broken down. The pundits affirmed that the bad
going after the rain had found them out. Allegedly the
selectors had taken a calculated risk in choosing two horses
with doubts; but as was pointed out, one of the horses that
were suspect had no problems. Had the going not been so
treacherous – it could hardly have been anticipated, as rain, we
were assured, was not usually expected in Bromont in July –
all our horses would have stood up to it and, even allowing for
Goodwill's fall we would have won the team silver. Almost
certainly Lucinda would have won an individual medal.

But suppose Goodwill had not fallen. Admittedly the
reasoning is somewhat hypothetical, just as it was making out
a case for Ann Moore winning the gold in Munich, but it
seems reasonable to suggest that Princess Anne's unlucky fall
at Fence 19 cost her a place in the top six. If the time faults
collected for the minutes that she lay on the ground
unconscious and the sixty penalty points for the fall are
deducted from her final score then it will be seen that even if
one assumed that she had the same time penalties as, say,
Lucinda or Richard – the low fifties – then her score at the end
of the cross-country would have taken her very near the top.
Then, having achieved one of the twelve clear rounds in the
show jumping, she must have finished very close to a medal.
She would have returned from the Montreal Olympics a
heroine. Instead, as was so often her lot in those days, she had
to read in the press of her 'failure', of her 'falling off', the
implication even being that she had been selected only because
she was the Queen's daughter. She must have found it
somewhat galling after her traumatic experience; but there
was one incident of light relief, which I am sure would have
amused her had she been aware of it. So unaccustomed were
the locals to a three-day event that on cross-country day

hundreds settled themselves to watch from the stands, unaware that, apart from the first fence on the steeplechase course, the riders went nowhere near the stands!

If there was a touch of Wagner during the closing stages of the cross-country in Mexico, it was almost *Gottedamerung* itself at the end of the individual show jumping at Bromont. There was a watery sunshine when the event started at 8.00 a.m. over Tom Gayford's big course built on sand. The first rider, Australia's Barry Roycroft, son of three-day event rider, Bill, was eliminated; the next Marc Roquet had 36 faults; Takeda for Japan had 33. Ninth to come in was Peter Robeson on Law Court. He had only ridden this brilliant horse, Law Court, owned by Andrew Massarella, for a few weeks, but faulting only at the treble, the penultimate fence, he went into the lead. For the experts' information the distances between the elements were 27 ft and 37 ft 6 in respectively, which caused considerable controversy. Poor Eric Wauters, for Belgium, collected 47.5 faults, in contrast to Michael Vaillancourt, his team-mate's four. For Canada, the home country, James Elder had eight, as did Jim Day. Graham Fletcher on old Hideaway had 20, while Debbie Johnsey, only nineteen years old, had a brilliant round on the 17 hh, eleven-year-old Moxy, for just 4 faults. One but last to go, Alwin Schockemohle achieved the only clear of the first round on the great Warwick Rex. This meant that both Peter Robeson and Debbie Johnsey qualified for the second round over an even bigger course which certainly took its toll. There were three eliminations; even the great Hans Winkler on Trophy had 16 faults, while the two Canadians, James Elder and Jim Day had 20 faults apiece – the same number as Peter Robeson on Law Court. But his were collected in a crashing fall at the treble when Law Court missed his stride at the last element; he also had 3¾ time faults. Debbie had another wonderful round with just two fences down, one very unluckily. This put her equal with Francois Mathy and Michel Vaillancourt for France and Belgium respectively, with only Schockemohle to jump. He did another superb clear to clinch the gold. As he did so the first drops of rain fell. In the distance could be heard rumbles of thunder: against the lowering black clouds over the mountains one could see the occasional vivid flash of lightning.

Within minutes a fantastic storm broke over the stadium. The rain came down vertically, the alarming flashes of lightning coinciding with the deafening crashes of thunder overhead. To no one's surprise and everyone's relief it was announced that the jump-off for the silver and bronze would be postponed until the storm had passed. Later this decision was questioned, it being a rule, apparently, in jumping under international rules that once a competition has started it must be finished or abandoned. Yet I seem to remember displays between the two rounds in a Nations Cup, even before a jump-off in a Grand Prix. As at Bromont it would have been quite impossible to continue jumping; had the event been abandoned the silver would have been shared by Debbie Johnsey, Vaillancourt and Mathy.

Rightly, though some felt that it was almost inhuman, Debbie's father insisted that she kept Moxy moving, riding around in the appalling storm, lest he stiffen up. When at one moment she attempted to shelter in a tent, the tent collapsed. And Debbie had celebrated her nineteenth birthday only three weeks earlier. No wonder her nerves were affected. Over a waterlogged course consisting of just six fences, she had the first fence down and stopped at the first element of the double for a total of $15\frac{1}{4}$. Thus she was robbed of a certain bronze, a possible silver, for all were agreed that her form was far more consistent than the not all that experienced Mathy and the unknown Vaillancourt. When I later met Alwin Schockemohle at a press reception he told me that he had been particularly fortunate that day because Warwick Rex could stand absolutely anything but rain on his back. Had his round been two minutes later he would have gone completely berserk. Was he just teasing? I would not be too sure. Debbie may have been even unluckier than she realised.

The last three Olympics had been at places beginning with the letter M: Mexico, Munich, Montreal. Each had spelt disaster for a very young British rider; Marion Mould, Ann Moore, Debbie Johnsey. Should it not have been M for misery? What on earth would happen in Moscow, the fourth M? We were, of course, ultimately spared the opportunity of finding out.

The weather had well and truly broken now. For the Grand

Prix de Dressage held over the next two days it was blustery and showery which must have made it very difficult for the participants. The BBC, not for the last or first time, did not show any great interest in the dressage so I found myself with two virtually free days which amongst other things gave me the chance to get better acquainted with two important visitors who, like me, were not over-occupied. One was Ian Trethowan, the Head of BBC 1, shortly to become Director General; the other was George Howard, Chairman of the Governors, whose lovely home in Yorkshire, Castle Howard, was used for the filming of *Brideshead Revisited*. Not only was it helpful to get to know those for whom I was working, but both proved to be very pleasant company, which was most welcome, as I was left a good deal on my own while all my professional colleagues were working an eighteen-hour day. On one of the free days I went down to Quebec with Michael Clayton, Editor of *Horse and Hound*. It was an extremely enjoyable – and revealing – trip. Having for so long been brought up on the great blotches of pink spread all over the atlas I had not fully appreciated how independent countries were once they had become part of the Commonwealth, rather than part of an empire. Quebec, of course, was French-speaking and decidedly unfriendly to the British. Even in Montreal when I asked a policeman on point duty if he could direct us to the motorway which would take us to Quebec he ignored me until Michael suggested that I ask him in French; which I did, whereupon he directed me in perfect English!

Montreal and Quebec were totally different as, indeed, I later discovered were Calgary and Toronto. Without doubt Quebec is the most beautiful, and has the most character; but I will never understand how Wolfe's soldiers scaled those perpendicular heights!

It was during one of my brief visits to the dressage that I heard a rumour to the effect that it was quite possible that because of the wet conditions the final team jumping might have to be held at Bromont rather than in the main stadium. Further, that at 6 a.m. on the Friday morning, it was planned to try a horse over some fences in the stadium to see whether the going would be suitable or whether it would cut up too much. Naturally I felt obliged to report this to my producer,

Fred Viner, whose immediate reaction was to have a camera down there. I warned him that it was only a rumour, but he insisted, arranging for Bob Armstrong, BBC News leading cameraman, to go down with us at 5 a.m. on the Friday morning. When we arrived at the stadium we found it all locked up. After half-an-hour or so wandering around we found a security man at one small entrance, waiting for the cleaners. With some difficulty we persuaded him to let us in though he made it clear that he would be keeping his eye on us as he thought the story of the horse being brought in to jump sounded very phoney. It was an eerie experience, alone in that vast stadium with its 80,000 capacity and its weird curving, umbrella-like roof. Patiently we sat and waited, warming ourselves against the cold and drizzle with the flask of coffee that Fred had brought. Suddenly we saw, through the entrance tunnel, a large vehicle drive in. Was it a horse box? We could see only its roof, then its back end as it drew up by the entrance. Would a horse be unloaded? Were we about to witness this secret ploy that no one knew anything about, giving the BBC a scoop, similar to the filming of the terrorists at Munich? We waited, but nothing came out of the back; instead a horde of people appeared suddenly at the entrance, obviously having come out of the front. They were the cleaners disgorging from a double-decker bus! We hung about for another hour during which I probably became the only BBC commentator ever to have seen an Olympic stadium being cleaned: interesting enough, but not particularly edifying.

Nor, sadly, was the British team's performance in the final jumping particularly edifying. Not that one should have expected it to have been. Except for Debbie Johnsey, with Moxy, no member of our team had ever actually won a competition of any sort on the horse that he had been asked to partner at Montreal; Peter Robeson and Law Court, Graham Fletcher and Hideaway and Roland Fernyhough and Bouncer. Hideaway did as well as could be expected for 16 and 20 in the two rounds; Bouncer had a wonderful second round for 4 after 27 in the first; Peter Robeson, due to another misunderstanding with Law Court, had a second crashing fall – yet how often can one recall Peter having a fall on one of his own horses? One cannot entirely blame the selectors. Our team had to consist of amateurs, owners were reluctant to lend or lease good horses, had a number of possible horses went lame before the Olympics. In the end Britain finished seventh out of eight. It was, as expected, a big course; the going was bad. There was no single clear round in the whole competition. France eventually won with a total of 40, beating Germany and Belgium with 44 and 63 respectively. Thirty-four faulted at the water out of the 53 who jumped it in the two rounds: 39 faulted at the last fence, a double consisting of a vertical at 4 ft 11 in and an oxer, also 4 ft 11 in, 5 ft 7 in wide. There were 26 ft between the two elements. The 1976 Olympics were the first for forty years in which Britain had not won any medal at all in the equestrian events.

As I had been working for the BBC for twenty-five years I had decided to retire after the Montreal Olympics, but with such a disappointing result I was relieved to be persuaded to stay on until after the Moscow Olympics, four years hence: surely we would do better in Moscow, indeed could hardly do worse. My only doubt concerned the security. It had irked me in Montreal and having experienced it once in Russia I did not particularly look forward to repeating the experience. Oddly enough when Mr Bobilov, who was to be in charge of the equestrian events in Moscow, held a press conference before we left Bromont he was, as can be imagined, asked a number of provocative and penetrating questions, all of which he answered honestly and often with a dry wit. Eventually a wag – could it have been Brian Giles from the *Daily Mail*? – asked him if the security in the Moscow Olympics would be very oppressive. Yes, said Mr Bobilov gravely, yes, security would be very strict, often frustrating; then he added with a hint of a twinkle in his eye, 'almost as strict and frustrating as in Montreal'. Security was obviously the name of the game in future Olympics.

In fact, Montreal did prove to be my swan song as far as the Olympics were concerned, which made an amusing incident at the end of the individual jumping particularly appropriate. After the first round of the individual jumping at Bromont there was a breakdown in the television – seemingly an almost inevitable Olympic experience for me – resulting in the commentators all having to dash back to the studios in

Montreal, commentating 'off the tube', each commentator being confined to a very small cubicle. When at the end of the transmission, which lasted nearly 2½ hours because of the delay due to the storm, I staggered out, gasping, exhausted, perspiring, I was surprised that as other commentators came out of their cubicles a number of them dashed up to me, thanking me profusely in various languages. Eventually I asked my BBC colleague, Peter Marsh, what on earth was happening. Why was I being thanked? What for? He then explained that there had not been time to tell me, but as many of the commentators had never previously commentated on show jumping the producer had arranged for my commentary to be fed into their ear-phones so that they could translate what I was saying into their own languages! Needless to say, I received no remuneration for this! But as I said to Peter, it seemed a pity that I was not then retiring as I could hardly have had a better send-off than the enthusiastic thanks of my fellow commentators.

Happily, I continued to work for the BBC for another four years; but missed Moscow, of course.

Calgary
Within a short time I was to revisit Canada twice. In February 1983 I was invited to give the principal talk at Calgary University's Equine Symposium. It was to be based on my book, *Great Riding Schools of the World*, which had been published in 1975, in the United States as well as in Britain, Germany and France. About 500 people attended the symposium which included a series of talks on such topics as hormones and horses, genetic designs of coat-colour, infectious diseases that affect reproduction in the mare, processed forage, lungeing and basic training, all contributed by experts from America or Canada. I was also asked to give a talk on the mind of the horse. Each speaker had to give his lecture twice in one of the small halls, those attending choosing which talk they wanted to go to, and when, over the three days. It is a pity that such a symposium cannot be held in Britain. At the end of the conference the Chairman, Professor Ron Cole, kindly invited me to stay a few days at his ranch or stud at Cochrane about thirty miles north-west of Calgary. He is a bachelor and lives a somewhat spartan existence – each evening we used to

buy our supper at a supermarket on the way home, I insisting
on a bottle of wine! – but with the help of an excellent young
assistant he runs an attractive little stud, and is obviously
devoted to his horses. He is also very musical; in his youth he
very nearly decided on a career as a professional pianist.
Altogether it was a most enjoyable and interesting three days
with a visit to Banff and a flight over the foothills of the
Rockies. We also went to Spruce Meadows where about ten
years ago Ron and Mary Southern founded a show-jumping
complex not unlike Hickstead. Here they now hold Canada's
principal international show, and in 1984 offered the richest
prize money in the world, with a Grand Prix worth $40,000 to
the winner. Strangely enough not only did the chief executive
of the Alberta Equestrian Federation, which generously
entertained me on the last day of my visit, come from England,
but also her sister-in-law had regularly taken part in the early
Shakespeare Festivals at Pendley. Her name was Jean Driver.

Later in the year I was invited to judge at the Royal Winter
Fair, Toronto; but more of that in a later chapter. The east side
and the west side of Canada could be in totally different
countries; Vancouver and Quebec are, of course, over 3000
miles apart. Ironically, the west has the wealth but only a
limited population, while the east has a large population which
dominates the voting. While I was in Calgary there was a by-
election in Alberta which, against all predictions in the polls,
was won by an independent separatist. There is no doubt that
the west feels very bitter at their limited representation in
Parliament. I was told in no uncertain terms that the Olympic
Games should have been held in the wealthy and fast-expand-
ing Calgary rather than in old-fashioned Montreal. In fact, the
city of Calgary covers a larger area than any other city on the
North American continent, even larger than Los Angeles
(which covers seventy square miles): but it seemed to me that,
apart from a square mile in the centre of the city, Calgary
straggled over acres and acres with bungalows and one storey
buildings in a somewhat haphazard manner: but it was,
perhaps, the informality of Calgary, stretching almost to the
foothills of the Rockies, that made it so attractive. One day, I
believe the Olympic Games will go to Calgary. Certainly I
would enjoy a return visit.

Part II

Other Equestrian Assignments

Chapter 6

From Russia With Love

Kiev 1973

Bob Dean, who, as Chairman of British Equestrian Promotions Ltd, the body that provides sponsors for the equestrian sports, has done so much for show jumping and eventing, chartered a British Airways plane to take supporters to the Three-Day Event European Championships at Kiev in September, 1973. The BBC and the equestrian press decided to take advantage of this, so on 4 September I found myself flying to Kiev. As always seemed to be the case, we had just finished the Pendley Shakespeare Festival with a production of *Hamlet* to celebrate our twenty-fifth year. *Hamlet* is always a challenge, but on this occasion it was a particular challenge for me, as it was only in July that I had had, after seven weeks of enervating and painful treatment, an operation for cancer. Naturally I was tired, but the five or six-hour flight was a rest-cure in itself. First-class conditions: champagne and caviar on take-off, an excellent four-course lunch.

We arrived at Kiev at about 6.00 p.m. and were driven to our hotel, the Dnipru. The party was only forty strong, but it took us well over an hour to get to our rooms, which were adequate rather than luxurious. At the end of each landing sat a formidable lady who took charge of our keys. Most of us were ready for a drink, but the bar did not open until 8.30 p.m. One could pay for one's drinks only in foreign currency, anything but roubles, which, of course, was helpful as far as we were concerned.

Next morning we were driven out to the Exhibition Centre of the Cultural and Economic Achievements of the Soviet Socialist Republic – no less – where the dressage and show jumping were being held. It was a fine day, which enabled us

to see something of the city at its best. One could not help but
be impressed. The streets were wide, clean and colourful with
flower beds, shrubs and trees: over three million trees have
been planted since the war, giving an impression that the city
has been built in a forest. Particularly effective was the
profusion of red creeper, Virginia or something similar, that
hung by official decree from every single window-box in
every massive apartment block. There are virtually no private
houses, few cars. To buy a car one has to wait anything from
three to seven years. Kiev certainly turned out to be a beautiful
city, either side of the great river Dneiper which wound its
way gently through the city. With a population of one and a
quarter million it is the third largest city in the Soviet
Republic. The people wore bright-coloured clothes, producing an almost festive impression. The attitude of the
Ukranians could best be described as cautiously friendly, for
Kiev is, of course, a Ukranian city which was absorbed into
Russia only after the 1917 revolution; but, as our Russian
television producer told us on one occasion when we were
driving out to the Exhibition Centre, there has, over the years,
been a steady influx of Russians so that now probably one in
three of the population is Russian, 'and it is necessary to be
cautious'. It was significant that he could tell us this only in the
privacy of his car. He would never have spoken in such a way
in his office; indeed he was quite a different person in his office
– very much the formal and rather evasive bureaucrat.

The lengthy Opening Ceremony took place on the Wednesday afternoon, with a number of speakers: Vladimin
Gusev, Chairman of the Executive Committee of the Soviet
Workers Deputies; Pavel Paryshev, Chairman of the USSR
Equestrian Sport Federation; the Duke of Edinburgh,
President of the FEI. There were frequent interruptions for
presentations of bouquets or lengthy interpretations or
impressive performances of various national anthems. One
part of Prince Philip's address seemed to me particularly
relevant: 'For a short time the real problems of the world,
floods and famine, politics and pollution, economics and
ecology, race and religion, will be forgotten in common
worship of man's oldest friend and ally in the animal king-
dom, the horse.'

His words were brought vividly to mind three days later when practically every paper in the world was concerned less with politics and the problems of the world than with Fence 2 on the cross-country course.

It was a fine warm day when we walked the course. The steeplechase course, which was at Zhuljari near the Exhibition Centre, was interesting in that it was similar to Mexico with walls, solid timber, open ditches. Most horses negotiated them satisfactorily, but only after the course had been disc-harrowed at the insistence of the *chefs d'equipe*. The roads and tracks linking the steeplechase with the cross-country consisted of a straight six-mile track to the area of the People's Architecture Museum. It even crossed a main road, which meant that all the traffic had to be held up every five minutes while a competitor trotted across.

The first fence on the cross-country, called an oxer, but in effect a solid trough encased in timber, was fairly innocuous, but Fence 2 – ! Officially it was described as Figure Farm which seemed meaningless. In fact it was a set of very solid parallels, 3 ft wide over an extremely deep ditch; so deep in fact that more than one competitor dropped down into the ditch, rode down it and climbed up the bank. Had this obstacle been set up in the middle of a field it would have created no great problem. It was the approach that made it so difficult. Coming round the side of a little hill on an uneven track – or going straight over the top as Richard Meade did – a horse had only five or, at the most, six strides in which to acquire sufficient impulsion to jump this daunting fence.

Not surprisingly there was something approaching an uproar from those walking the course. Many, in fact, never got beyond it. Most blame was attached to the technical delegate, the Argentine Pedro Mayorga whose course for the European Championships at Punchestown in Ireland in 1967 had been the target for much criticism. But he was not prepared in any way to modify the fence, nor any other of the thirty fences; though, to be fair, the rest of the course was comparatively straightforward, apart from the fact that being so undulating it made it a severe test for any horse.

When the first of the forty-three competitors started the cross-country at 10.00 a.m. on the Saturday morning there

was already a vast crowd at Fence 2, but this, it turned out, was
not because of the severity or interest of the fence, but because
it was the only fence in view of the television cameras – the
only two cameras on the course. To give the impression that
the event was well attended the authorities had 'recruited' a
crowd. This became apparent when a young Russian asked
one of our party what was supposed to be happening. When he
had arrived at work that morning he was simply told that he
was not working that day but was to go on a coach ride. Two
hours later he found himself on the bank above Fence 2
together with perhaps a thousand other Russians who had
arrived there in the same way. It was 11.45 a.m. when the first
competitor reached Fence 2, and very hot; although one's
perspiration was as much due to anxiety and anticipation.
Appropriately the first competitor to arrive was a Russian,
Yuri Salnikov, his instructions as pathfinder, we understood
later, being to go flat out from the start. At Fence 2 his horse
just managed to keep his feet despite his belly at one moment
being on the ground: shortly afterwards he had a fall
somewhere in the wood, finally sinking without trace at the
water, named the Trout Hatchery; and taking no further part
in the event. I, for one, did not blame him. If one hurried, it
was just possible to reach the Trout Hatchery, having seen the
same rider over Fence 2. Of the next four riders, two had really
horrible falls at the second fence, two were eliminated. Then
came Richard Meade on Wayfarer who came straight over the
top of the hill, attacked the trakhener really fast and cleared it
comparatively easily. Unfortunately he was to have a stop at
the Trout Hatchery attempting to jump sideways on to the
bank avoiding the deep water in the middle.

Only three of the eleven riders between Richard Meade and
Princess Anne survived without a fall or elimination at Fence
2. Princess Anne, riding Goodwill, not as a member of the
team but as an individual, was due to start the cross-country at
1.20 p.m. By this time the crowd at Fence 2 was huge, leaving
practically nobody for any other fence, other than those who
rushed across to the Trout Hatchery for each competitor –
each competitor, that is, that had survived Fence 2, which was
well under 50 per cent. Had Princess Anne been able to steady
Goodwill as she did three years later in Montreal at the second

fence there, the trakhener would have presented no problem,
but the immensely powerful Goodwill took off a full stride too
early. He so very nearly made it, but, just catching a hind leg
on the back pole, he crashed to the ground, giving his rider a
heavy fall. Sensibly, not being a member of the team, but
having been entered as an individual, Princess Anne retired, so
forfeiting her chance of retaining her European Championship
which she had won at Burghley on Doublet two years earlier;
and in which she was to come second two years later. It might,
however, be added that it was additionally unfortunate for
Princess Anne in that she had had to tackle the largest part of
the fence, on the left-hand side; the centre, where it was
slightly lower, had been made unsafe by the bank crumbling
where horses had slid into the ditch.

Princess Anne had been due to finish the course at 1.45 p.m.
I had been instructed to meet my producer, Fred Viner, by the
score-board at 1.50 p.m., to be driven straight into Kiev
where we could put out a programme which could be slotted
into BBC's 'Grandstand'. As soon as I had seen Princess Anne
safely on her feet I set off for the score-board. As my ankles
were rather swollen, the result of my operation and spending
so much time on my feet rehearsing *Hamlet* at Pendley, I had
brought an old pair of soft suede shoes to wear in Kiev.
Unfortunately they had leather soles which, as I had stupidly
failed to appreciate, made walking on dry grass very difficult.
Sure enough climbing up the bank above Fence 2 I slipped and
fell. Thanks to my slippery soles and my weakness at that time
– enhanced by my frequent dashes in the intense heat from
Fence 2 to the Trout Hatchery – I was quite unable to rise.
There I lay helpless. Whether it was just unfriendliness or
whether it was assumed that I was drunk I do not know, but it
was very much a case of 'passing by on the other side'. No one
wanted to help me; my struggles were in vain. I was getting
desperate: I seemed to be lying there for minutes – I prayed
that Fred who knew that I had been at Fence 2 would come and
find me. Eventually I plucked up the courage to seize a man's
leg. He stopped, looked down at me in a surly manner, was
about to shake me off and continue on his way when with my
free hand I pointed to my torso. Probably he thought that I
was demonstrating a heart condition. At any rate, roughly he

helped me up to my feet, his expression making it all too clear
what he thought of the effete English.

I was exhausted when I met Fred, but it was only 1.45 p.m.:
I had not kept him waiting. We jumped into our car, reached
the studio, five miles away, by 2.15 p.m. and within ten
minutes I was dubbing my commentary on the film of
Princess Anne's fall. The 'Grandstand' transmission from
Hickstead was interrupted to show the up-to-the-minute but
unhappy news from Kiev. As one might have expected, the
BBC was more excited at this scoop in showing Princess
Anne's fall within an hour of it happening than the effect that it
had on Princess Anne, or the fortunes of the British team.

As our next rider, Debbie West on Baccarat, was on the
course while we were in the car we did not know what
happened to her, but when we saw on television in the studio
Janet Hodgson on Larkspur continue after their horrific fall at
Fence 2 we guessed that Debbie must have been eliminated, as
she had been. Janet, of course, appreciated that however badly
hurt she was, she now had to finish the course if Britain were
not to be eliminated. Despite another fall at some parallels she
managed to complete the course. We were back on the course
for our last rider, the nineteen-year-old Lucinda Prior-Palmer
with Be Fair. Thanks to advice from Richard Meade and Bill
Lithgow, the *chef d'equipe*, that she should 'get my bat out and
ride really strongly at Fence 2, keeping my horse going', she
did just that and 'was extremely thankful when Be Fair
managed it with just a peck on landing', which would have
caused most riders to fall off, but Lucinda never moved.
Unfortunately three fences further on, an imposing log pile,
she did have an uncharacteristic fall. Many people would have
blamed inadequately controlled spectators wandering around,
but Lucinda insisted that 'we just got it wrong'.

Although Britain's final score at the end of the second day
was 525 penalty points it was good enough for us to be lying
third behind West Germany, the only team to get all four
riders home, with 350 penalty points, and Russia with 471.

That evening, though I was really too tired to enjoy it, we
were taken out to a Pectomah – an up-market municipal
restaurant – in a forest. It was more like a refined holiday camp
which specialised in traditional Ukranian meals; ours

consisted of a spoonful of caviar, salami and a pork chop, washed down with vodka, which we had to buy, small groups sharing a bottle. There was a band and dancing, but to persuade it to play after 11.00 p.m. we had to have a whip round and bribe them in English pounds and American dollars, the only other party that evening coming from Chicago. At 11.15 p.m. officials arrived and insisted on the immediate closing of the Pectomah.

The one topic of conversation, of course, was the cross-country, in particular Fence 2. Most people were very critical. In a report that I wrote at the time I said: 'Obviously events of this standard and importance have to be severe and demanding. A sub-standard course can produce freak results, which nobody wants. But I am of the opinion that a wholly acceptable result could have been achieved without the appalling toll taken by Fence 2 – a fence which could easily have been modified by the technical delegate, secondly, that an event with this sort of gladiatorial atmosphere does the sport no good.' By mid-afternoon there had scarcely been any crowd at all; the spectators had just had enough, as had even the pressmen and photographers. One correspondent in his report wrote: 'In the three-day event we are looking for horses and riders with courage, ability, stamina: not volunteers for suicide squads.'

With West Germany holding such a large lead – they could have ten fences down and still beat the Russians – as far as the team event was concerned the show-jumping phase was of only academic interest; in fact they increased their lead thanks to a disastrous round by the Russian Vladimir Soroka. The individual result was exciting in that Alexander Evdokimov, who was narrowly in the lead after the cross-country, had a fence down in the show jumping which brought him down to equal with West Germany's Herbert Blocker who had been standing second: but the Russian was awarded the gold having had the fastest time across country. All the British team riders had clear rounds, as did Rosemary Jones riding as an individual; Margery Comerford, another individual rider, also had one fence down, which dropped her from third to fifth and cost her the individual bronze. In most people's opinion Britain should have won the silver. The Russian

Soroka stopped at the first fence and he had another refusal at a
little water jump. Then, as I made very clear on television, he
circled before jumping it. This, of course, should have eliminated him, and with him the whole Russian team as they had
already lost their fourth rider, Salnikov. Led by an American
girl, who had been penalised at the previous Burghley Horse
Trials for circling, various nations which were not in any way
involved persuaded the British *chef d'equipe* to lodge an objection. It was over-ruled, which may have been just as well as it
would not have been very tactful for Britain to have been
placed second at the expense of our hosts, especially as the
premier, Mr Brezhnev himself, was present. (I had the
privilege of shaking hands with him, but he spoke to me
neither in Russian, nor English; nor I to him.) Had it been
possible for the jury to see a recording of the incident there is
no doubt that Soroka would have been eliminated; but there
was no way that they could have seen a recording as it was, I
can honestly say, the worst television with which I have ever
been associated. The camera wandered all over the place and
was seldom able to pick up a horse. They did have Soroka's
circle, but they would never have been able to find it in the
recording.

Although only 20 horses out of 43 starters were involved in
the show jumping, the whole performance, including the
presentations, took over four hours. The one rewarding
moment was when, quite unexpectedly, Janet Hodgson was
presented with a magnificent gold pendant watch as 'a special
reward for courage': some compensation for her four missing
teeth.

We did not get back to Kiev until nearly seven o'clock, thus
missing the first half of a theatre visit that had been arranged
for us. The Ukranian dancers in gay, colourful costumes were
spectacular, while the acrobatic dancers were sensational. The
dining-room was closed by the time we reached Hotel
Dnipru, as was the bar.

Bob Dean had arranged for us to spend a couple of days in
Moscow before returning to England. Rightly he felt that
having come so far we should not miss the opportunity of
seeing Moscow and visiting the Kremlin, St Basil's Cathedral
and the Bolshoi Ballet. Like everyone else I was greatly

looking forward to it and could not wait to board our luxury
aircraft next morning for the ninety-minute flight to Moscow.

Moscow
Obligingly our coach driver on the way from the airport made
a slight diversion in order for us to see the remarkable statue
erected in honour of the astronauts. It is a leaning tower, 100 ft
high, surmounted by a silver rocket; from a distance it looks
like Concorde taking off. It was as impressive as anything I
saw in Moscow, which was as dreary as Kiev had been gay.
Our hotel, The Ocmahkuho, a totally characterless building,
was on the outskirts of Moscow. Again it took us over an hour
to register and find our rooms. The lift was only large enough
to take two people with their baggage – only one in the case of
'Babe' Moseley, who certainly had not lost any weight since
our trip to Stockholm seventeen years earlier. My room was
on the third floor, virtually a dormitory which I had to share
with Fred Viner, Alan Smith of the *Daily Telegraph*, Les Lane,
the photographer and another journalist. There was only one
lavatory on each floor to be shared by about twenty-five
people.

We were told to assemble in the foyer at 6.00 p.m. to be
driven into the centre of Moscow, twenty miles away, for
dinner, there being no dining facilities in the hotel. While we
were waiting for everyone to congregate, our Intourist guide,
an attractive young lady, outlined the plans for our visit. Not
surprisingly she was asked when we would be visiting the
Kremlin and what about our tickets for the Bolshoi.
Unfortunately, she told us, neither of those were possible as,
staying less than six nights, we were regarded as second-class
tourists. Second-class! 'Babe' Moseley's reaction was predict-
able. Second-class! Did she not realise, he squeaked in his
high-pitched voice, that our party included a number of
distinguished officers in the British Army? Second-class! We
even had the BBC with us! There was nothing second-class
about our party. To be referred to as second-class was an
insult. Others joined in. Why come to Moscow if you cannot
see the Kremlin? How else were we to see the Bolshoi unless
we saw it in Moscow as the Russians were too afraid to let it
come to London? Whose idea, anyway, was it that we were

housed in this prison block? At first the young lady attempted
to explain, then as the questioning became more aggressive
she became tearful. Weakly I suggested that she was only
doing her duty. Bravely she said that unless we set off in the
coach immediately we would not get any dinner at all as the
Pectomah closed early and our coach was only hired until
8.00 p.m. As we clambered on to the coach the poor young
lady was informed in no uncertain terms that if she thought we
were going to drive the twenty miles to Moscow, have a meal
and return to our hotel, all by 8.00 p.m. she was much
mistaken. Somehow it transpired during our drive that the
driver would be open to a bribe. How much? For £60 he
would wait until we had finished our meal, then drive us to
Red Square before taking us back to the hotel. We forked up.

The Pectomah was huge, something of a poor man's
Grosvenor House, with seating for 2000. Our party sat
together at one table and had an adequate but not very
inspiring meal. The Red Square, floodlit, under a full moon
was certainly inspiring. Completely opposite to the stark
simplicity of the Astronauts' Memorial it was a Russian fairy
tale with all its colour and contrasts. It was about 11.00 p.m.
when we returned to the hotel with strict instructions that the
coach would leave at exactly 8.00 a.m. next morning to take
us to the Pectomah for breakfast.

An unfortunate but not unusual result of the major operation that I had had in July was the necessity of visiting the
lavatory four or five times every night. As Fred Viner and I
were sleeping in the inner sanctum of our dormitory I had to
walk through the larger room to get to the door. Not wishing
to disturb my dormitory companions I did not turn on the
light as there was sufficient moonlight to enable me to find my
way. Each time I tripped over one of the wooden blocks that
formed the somewhat crude parquet floor. In the morning I
apologised for any disturbance that this may have been caused
which encouraged one of our group to inspect the cause of the
trouble.

'As one might have expected', he said. Underneath the
wooden block was a crude bugging device. If it was working
and if anyone was listening they would have heard little to
their advantage!

Not surprisingly we were not a full complement when we were due to leave at 8.00 a.m. on the coach. Despite protestations by our Intourist guide the party insisted on waiting for the last two ladies, who had, in fact, kept us waiting on practically every occasion since the beginning of our trip. It was 9.00 a.m. when we arrived at the Pectomah. Our breakfast had been ordered at 8.45 a.m., so at 8.45 a.m. the toast and the boiled eggs had been put on our table. No amount of pressure would make the silent, sullen staff bring us fresh toast or replacements for our eggs. The plan was that we should be driven to the foreign currency shops where we were expected to spend three hours before being conveyed back to the Pectomah for lunch. Surely, we suggested, it must somehow be possible for us to see the Kremlin. The Intourist lady tactfully left the table. Within five minutes it was arranged that our coach would, by chance, 'break down' on the river bank at the entrance to the Kremlin. Would it cost us another £60? No, it would cost us £80.

We duly disgorged at the foot of the Kremlin and walked through to Red Square, having been instructed to reassemble at the coach at 12.30 p.m. We did not manage to penetrate the Armoury or see Lenin's tomb, but St Basil's Cathedral was imposing and one could not fail to be impressed by the sea of golden cupolas. There was time for a brief visit to a foreign currency shop where it seemed that prices were fixed at random. Bob Dean's wife, Lilian, and I both bought attractive little lacquered boxes, but whereas I paid £19 for mine she paid £25 for hers. In general the prices were not exorbitant. By 12.30 p.m. most of us had assembled by the coach, the two unpunctual ladies hurrying up last. Immediately they discovered something that had escaped the rest of us. Lawrie, our courier, was missing. We waited a few minutes before the Intourist lady set off to see if she could find him. She was soon back. At the little stone building at the entrance she learned that he had been arrested. But why on earth? What for? Apparently he was carrying a briefcase larger than the permissible size, which was not surprising, as inside it were all our tickets and some of our party's passports. The advice of the Intourist lady was that we should carry on, hoping that he would be released and return under his own steam to our

hotel. Could she, I wondered, be involved, either getting her
own back for the way we had treated her the previous night or
in an arrangement with the authorities for cheating that
morning with our coach?

The two unpunctual ladies proved to be sentimental as well
as unpunctual. We could not possibly leave without Lawrie,
they insisted. I could, and said so, whereupon a violent
argument broke out. To me, perhaps rather callously, it
seemed more realistic to carry on than risk the possibility of us
all being taken off for 'questioning'. Already the Intourist lady
was saying that the coach dared not wait any longer lest the
driver be arrested having 'illegally' taken us to the Kremlin.
To the suggestion that we would never be able to leave
Moscow without our tickets Bob Dean pointed out that as we
were all flying British Airways on British Airways tickets
there would be no problem. Finally, a little guiltily, somewhat
anxious, we all boarded the coach; all, that is, except the two
ladies who, displaying commendable courage and loyalty
remained behind, assuring us that they intended to stay until
they had found Lawrie, whom they would bring to the hotel.
We wished them well.

Our lunch at the Pectomah had been ordered for 1.00 p.m.
It was 1.30 when we arrived, but, as we had anticipated, the
tomato soup had been put on the table at precisely 1.00 p.m. It
did not matter that the salami or the ice cream were cold, but
we had to accept the fact that cold soup and tepid potatoes
were our lot. All efforts to obtain tickets for the Bolshoi Ballet
or any other entertainment failed. I was, too, refused permission to visit the National Equestrian Centre at Ismailova Park.
Somewhat disconsolately we returned to our hotel where we
found the two ladies, but no Lawrie; and the bar was closed.

It was with some trepidation that we eventually reached the
airport. Who should greet us there but Lawrie? He suggested
that the authorities had detained him to tease us, knowing that
we had, as second-class citizens, infringed the regulations. I
could not help wondering, however, if perhaps he had not
decided that he could spend a more enjoyable twenty-four
hours in Moscow without his second-class tourists; with the
attractive young Intourist lady, perhaps? Perish the thought! I
am sure that the two ladies were right when they asserted that

Lawrie would never do such a thing. But I am not sure that I would not have been tempted in his place. Anything to relieve the depressing grey drabness of Moscow. I certainly had no regrets at leaving it, the constant feeling of suspicion and oppression, the total lack of colour – apart from Red Square – in clothes and buildings and, I suspected, peoples' lives. Obviously it had been an interesting experience, even fascinating in retrospect, but by this time I only longed for home and our beautiful Foscote, where I could have the rest and relaxation that I had been looking forward to ever since the end of the Pendley Festival.

There was one amusing incident at the airport before we congregated in the departure lounge. As Mrs Derek Allhusen went over the little bridge, which tests passengers for the presence on their person of some metal object, the bell buzzed. She was stopped; relieved of her camera, she went through again. Again the bell buzzed. Her binoculars were taken away from her, then her umbrella – but still the buzz. Finally they took her handbag. The bell did not buzz. Smiles all round. Her bag was handed back to her and she continued on her way; but none of the security officers ever thought to look in her bag, so relieved were they that they had found which article it was that had caused the buzz!

Eventually we were airborne. The champagne flowed; everyone drank to a safe return to England. The two ladies toasted Lawrie. I just murmured to Fred Viner, sitting next to me: 'From Russia with love'.

Chapter 7

Blue Grass – For Free

Kentucky 1978

I was very surprised to learn that the BBC was not televising the World Three-Day Event Championships at Lexington, Kentucky, in September, 1978; and disappointed, too. However, there was some compensation when I was informed that they wanted me to be there as they might arrange one or two 'unilaterals'; in other words, if something particularly exciting happened involving a British rider they would want me to dub a commentary for British viewers over the coverage that NBC was producing. I might also be required for the occasional radio broadcasts. They suggested, therefore, that I should book myself on to the special charter flight being organised for *Horse and Hound* by Montpelier Travel. At the same time Michael Clayton, editor of *Horse and Hound*, had very kindly offered me a free place on the tour if I would act as leader. This meant that I was in the fortunate position of having two free tickets, which, of course, included full board during the eight days in Lexington, so Jennifer was able to come, too. Although I did not let it in any way spoil my trip I felt almost embarrassed by the end of the trip as the BBC had not required me for a single moment throughout the event, chiefly because the British team was eliminated on the cross-country; nor were my duties with the tour party exactly onerous as Michael Clayton was there all the time himself. We therefore had a memorable holiday in Kentucky at no cost whatever to ourselves.

The party left Gatwick in two DC8s on 12 September. Fortunately we were in the plane that left on time. The second plane was delayed four hours which was at least to the benefit of one passenger who had left her passport on the table by the front door in her flat in Bath. Fortunately, her son was able to get it there in time. We were supposed to fly direct to Louisville, but for some reason we came down at Pittsburg where we were delayed about three hours; this meant that we arrived at Hyatt Regency Hotel in Lexington at about ten o'clock in the evening instead of late afternoon. However, we were able to organise a light meal before retiring to bed very tired, as one always is after these long flights. (How *do* world statesmen conduct business of vital importance to humanity having flown half round the world?)

It was a bright, breezy morning when we woke up, with the first hints of autumn, or fall, which enabled us to explore a little of the town or, officially, the city (population 200,000). As it tends to straggle one did not get an impression of the size or the business of a city. We also learnt our way around the very lush Hyatt Regency Hotel with its pool, Jacuzzi, garden restaurant and, inevitably, coffee bar. Meanwhile, Michael was organising a hired car which would enable us to be independent rather than have to travel with the rest of the party by coach.

Inevitably our first move was to go to Lexington Horse Park which had only been opened on 15 July, just two months earlier, and acquaint ourselves with the press centre, team headquarters and the stable area. This took us until lunch-time, but restaurant facilities being very inadequate we contented ourselves with a hamburger and a Seven-Up; there were no bars. On a lovely fresh clear-skied afternoon we walked the course. Inevitably during our walk we met up with a number of competitors, trainers and the usual pundits who always seem to be attached unofficially to each team, ready at all times to proffer their advice and opinion, suggesting a wealth of not always authenticated experience. Opinion seemed to be divided as to the severity of the course. Some found it very straightforward; others felt that the most demanding fences, usually combinations, coming at the end of the course could cause trouble. Laurence Rook, whose opinion I have always respected, suggested that everything depended on the weather. How right he was to be proved! For myself, it all looked terrifying as usual. I was particularly surprised that not more people were concerned about the sixth fence, an enormously wide trakhener; but perhaps I remembered more vividly than most that trakhener at Stockholm in 1956.

There were only seven teams taking part, but the dressage was spread over two days, due to the number of individual American riders taking part. Jennifer and I extended the lunch break to explore a little more thoroughly the whole complex of this magnificent Horse Park. It had taken four years to complete – in fact it was not wholly completed. It had cost nearly fifty million dollars to construct in 1,000 acres of typical Kentucky rolling grassland. Its stadium was built to hold over 20,000 people; its exhibition hall covered 70,000 square feet. There were also jumping arenas, manèges, a restored opera house and a hotel (neither of the latter two being completed in 1978). At the centre of it all was the superb more-than-life-size bronze of America's perhaps most famous stallion, Man o' War, which won 20 of his 21 races, his only defeat being by a horse appropriately called Upset.

Instead of returning to the Horse Park for the second day of the dressage we joined the tour of the famous studs that had been organised. A few years earlier I had done the commentary on a fascinating film of the Blue Grass country made by James Hall. The opportunity to see it for myself alone made the trip to Kentucky worthwhile. Lexington is known as Queen of the Blue Grass country; certainly it is impossible to imagine more ideal pasture land than provided for no less than 1,000 horse farms that exist at Lexington within a radius of thirty-five miles. The exceptional quality of the land is reckoned to be due to the lime content. In the last fifty years on only one or two occasions has Kentucky failed to produce each year the nation's most successful sire. Even the names of some of the studs and farms make one thrill with anticipation, being, in addition, romantic and evocative: Spendthrift, Keeneland, Clayborne, Danada, Castleton, Darby Dan, Dixiana, Normandy, Greentree. Recently Murty Farm, 450 acres, was sold for £35,000 per acre, which is testimony to the value accorded to Blue Grass country.

There is a road in the Blue Grass country called Iron Works Pike. It is almost dead straight, about eight miles long. On either side there is nothing but a succession of beautiful, extensive, lavishly fenced paddocks belonging to some of the most famous studs in the world. We were fortunate enough to visit half a dozen of these including two of the most famous, Spendthrift and Clayborne. Almost the most impressive moment of our whole stay in Kentucky was when Nijinsky was paraded for our inspection at Spendthrift. To stand within a few feet of this most famous of all stallions, even to touch him, produced, as far as I was concerned, the kind of reaction that I had experienced touching the piece of John of Gaunt's surcoat at Badminton, or sitting in the chair which Charlotte Brontë used when writing *Jane Eyre*: one felt one was in contact with history at first hand.

The most remarkable of all the studs was Clayborne, where some thirty-eight stallions, each looking immaculate, stand in well-ordered yards. No mares are on the premises at all; they come in from anything up to a hundred miles away, are served in the mating centre which, with all its efficiency, cleanliness, hygiene, can be compared to a hospital, even to an operating theatre, although with the non-stop arrival and departure of mares, the regular production of the required stallion, it could be likened more to a factory. The whole complex was built up from absolutely nothing by a remarkable man who appeared to be the very epitome of the American rags-to-riches story.

Jennifer, a perfectionist herself, and properly critical, felt, to her surprise, that some of the studs, including one of the best known, left something to be desired in both horsemastership and stud management. But all of us were impressed, from a sentimental point of view, with the very plebean grey cat that shared permanently a box with one of the most eminent and valuable French bred stallions in the world. It was a memorable experience, made all the more delightful by the perfect weather.

When we woke next morning, Saturday, it was obvious that the weather had changed. The clear skies were now overcast, but with mist rather than cloud. It was sultry, humid, oppressive. The queues approaching the Horse Park suggested a large crowd. 50,000 had been anticipated, but it was later announced that over 70,000 had attended. On more than one occasion we were grateful for our press passes, even if I felt something of a fraud being in possession of them for, as can be imagined, they were eagerly sought after. We spent the two or three hours before the first horse reached the cross-country phase walking some of the course again, inspecting the worst of the fences. We had not walked very far before we realised the effect of the humidity. We were quickly exhausted and breathless.

We decided to start watching at Fence 6, the huge trakhener. The first competitor to reach it, Carlos Ramson of Argentina, stopped but got over at the third attempt. The second, Sumatra, ridden by Juliet Bishop of Canada, cleared it, but three of the next four were in trouble, and then an American rider astonished everybody by not jumping it at all. He slithered down into the ditch, crept along the ditch under the pole to its full length before clambering out up the bank and popping over the pole at the top. This, of course, was the way to do it; and as a rider doing this was at all times between the flags it was quite legitimate. Major Derek Allhusen, individual silver medalist in Mexico, who was watching at this fence, managed to get a message back to Lucinda Green who, with Village Gossip, would be starting in about twenty minutes. Cleverly she achieved the fiddle, carrying on brilliantly, until she reached the Serpent, a three-fence combination at the end of the course, where she came to grief because, in her own words, 'we were going faster than we should'. A fence with a very big ditch was followed by a zig-zag over a brook approached at an angle of ninety degrees. At one moment, halfway through the event, seven consecutive riders came to grief at the Serpent. It could well have been more had it not been for the prompt action by a spectator. That spectator happened to be none other than the President of the FEI, Prince Philip. As he told me later that evening, he was well aware that he was breaking the rules, but he felt that his action was justified. He doubted, too, that anyone would question his action. When he saw horse after horse crashing at the zig-zag over the brook he realised that it was because the bank was collapsing, just as at Stockholm, and the approach was not only becoming very slippery, but also shelving as more and more earth collapsed into the brook. He immediately ordered a load of shale to be spread over the approach. The rules are, of course, that conditions shall be exactly the same for every competitor; but there is no doubt that his action saved further casualties, possibly a fatal one.

The Serpent was made worse in that it followed immediately the water complex, known as the Head of the Lake. Having jumped a double into the lake, competitors then had to leap up on to quite a high bank out of fairly deep water. Crossing the bank they then jumped a considerable flight of rails back into the water with a steep drop. Finally they had to wade through more water and jump out on to rising ground at the end of the water. Fifty yards further on there was a set of rails at the top of the hill. Jane Holderness Roddam came to grief here. The horse, appearing to be exhausted already, fell jumping up onto the bank. Jane remounted, clambered up, but jumping the rail back into the water Warrior caught a hind leg on the rail, pitching Jane into the water. With great courage she carried on, but with good sense retired when she reached the Serpent; Warrior had had enough. As Jack le Goff, for many years the American three-day event team's trainer, said, 'That water took a lot out of the horses, it really got their batteries flat.' Already the horses had had to cope with some very undulating terrain leading up to the Old Fort Lexington, similar to Badminton's Normandy Bank, but bigger. There were many falls here including Martha Anne Shires of Canada and Chris Collins on Smokey, who it was felt, with hindsight, had gone too fast over the early part of the course in view of the fact that these demanding combinations came at the end when the humidity would almost certainly have had its effect.

This humidity, undoubtedly, was the villain of the piece. It is not, I understand, unknown in Kentucky for there to be high humidity in September. In designing the course, was sufficient allowance made? In the opinion of many it was not; Le Goff likened the event to a battlefield. 'There were too many combinations', he said. 'In conditions like this one effort after another takes it out of a horse. There was no time that one could relax.' Before the event he had described the cross-country course as 'both a horse course and a rider course', by which he meant that 'the horse would have to use itself to get round and the rider would have to use his head to help his horse'. Later he was to insist that Lexington was the toughest course he had ever seen, without allowing for the high humidity; 'and I've been to every course in the world, both as a rider and a trainer.' Statistics are significant: four of the 7 teams were eliminated; 26 riders out of the 46 had falls; 20 were eliminated; 9 horses alone fell at the Serpent, apart from all the refusals.

Course builder, Roger Haller, who had taken three years planning the course, was, however, unrepentant. The trouble with the Serpent, he explained, was that riders foolishly took tired horses the short and most difficult way. Riders on less experienced horses who went the long way made it look easy. He had, he said, no sympathy for those who complained. As far as I was concerned the whole argument was settled by the experience we witnessed at the end of Bruce Davidson's round on the comparatively inexperienced Might Tango. At the end of the cross-country course the horse was in a state of complete exhaustion, staggering like a drunken man; indeed, it had to be supported by grooms and others while cold water was splashed over it and an ice pack held to its head. Finally Dr Kert Vasco, a veterinary surgeon, not officially connected with the Championships, administered oxygen, and the horse eventually, after an hour or so, recovered. To my astonishment it was allowed to continue in the competition, and took part in the show jumping next day, duly winning the individual gold medal. It had not apparently in any way infringed the rules. Perhaps it would have been better if it had.

Canada went into the final day with a lead of 105.6 points and easily won the team medal – another of their welcome, unexpected victories, such as when they won the gold medal in the Mexico Olympics show jumping. It was all the more commendable in that, as Mike Herbert, their English trainer, pointed out, they had no problems in selecting their teams as they went to Kentucky with the only four horses they had left. Significantly they had, apparently, specifically trained in heat.

It was all excellently organised and, as always, a thoroughly interesting experience; but I do not think that I was the only one who wondered whether top-level eventing could survive another cross-country phase with so much disaster – in particular with so much stress – even among the most experienced horses.

On the Saturday evening we were invited to a big reception at an imposing State House where there was a barbeque. Julian

M. Carroll, the forty-ish, charismatic Governor of Kentucky, made a speech of welcome to which I was called upon to reply; but whether it was as Chairman of British Horse Society, leader of the *Horse and Hound* tour, or as senior BBC commentator who had not had an opportunity so far to say a word, I do not know. Nevertheless, we enjoyed ourselves – as indeed we had enjoyed all the typical American hospitality. We departed from Louisville on our return flight on time, but for some reason we had to wait four hours at Pittsburg – an unscheduled stop again – before eventually boarding our plane. Allegedly we were waiting for a plane to arrive from Tokyo. Finally we took off at 1.30 a.m., arriving at Gatwick somewhat jaded, but, thanks to the BBC and *Horse and Hound*, having enjoyed an extremely pleasant eight days. It was probably the cheapest holiday we had ever had: though an earlier visit to the States had also cost me personally nothing, but my hosts a great deal more. This, in turn, followed a brief, unexpected visit a few years previously.

Los Angeles 1968
Jennifer and I intended on our way back from Melbourne in 1966, where we had been judging at the Royal Show, to spend a few days at Acupulco. Unfortunately there was a strike on Quantas Airlines which ruled out our plans as the British Airways flights did not fit in with our dates. We, therefore, decided to call in on Los Angeles, although everyone had told us that we should avoid it if we possibly could. On our flight out to Australia a neighbour on the plane had been a young teacher who worked in San Francisco but who lived in Los Angeles. With typical American hospitality he insisted that if ever we were in Los Angeles we must look him up and allow him to show us around. He even wrote his name and address on the menu and drew a map of the area in which he lived, and in addition listed names of good restaurants in case he should be in San Francisco while we were in Los Angeles. Naturally we never expected to see or hear of him again, but when our plans had to be altered in Melbourne I dropped him a card giving him the number of our flight and the time of arrival, just on the slender chance that he would still be in Los Angeles and, if he was, would get our card in time.

He was and he did, appearing to be delighted that we had taken him at his word. He had booked us in, he told us, at four different hotels. He would drive us to each of them and we could then choose which one we preferred. Having made our choice we invited him to stay and dine with us, but he insisted on leaving us as he knew that we would be tired after our long flight from Melbourne, which, of course, was true. However, he assured us that he would phone us next morning and, if we wished it, would drive us round to see the sights.

Both in his company and on our own we spent a very rewarding three or four days in Los Angeles which, not surprisingly, made a most favourable impression on us, the more so, perhaps, because we were actually staying in Santa Monica. To see the legendary Hollywood and Beverly Hills, and even a film set, was quite an experience, especially with someone who seemed to know his way around so well.

On the last evening that we were there we decided to take out to supper a girl called Gill Ansell; she had at one time worked for us and now had a good job in Los Angeles looking after a sizeable stable. Naturally we asked our friend if he could recommend a rather special restaurant, and felt that the least that we could do was to ask him to join us so that we could repay a little of his hospitality. After a drink in the hotel he took us to an enchanting restaurant down on the wharf, all the decor being like the deck of a fishing vessel. The food was excellent. When it was time for us to return to our hotel – he had kindly offered to drive us home via the district where Gill lived – I asked for the bill. To my great embarrassment I found that he had already settled it and despite my protests refused to allow me to refund him. I was most embarrassed. Not only had I asked him to choose a really high-class restaurant but had inflicted upon him a total stranger, albeit a very attractive one. On top of it all he took it for granted that he would be driving us to the airport the following morning although we had to leave the hotel at 6.30 a.m. An example of American hospitality at its best.

We kept in touch for a while but although he said that he would contact us when he came to England he never did. Nor was there any reply to my letter when I told him that I was visiting Los Angeles again. Probably he had settled in San Francisco.

Los Angeles had made a much better impression on us than we had anticipated, so it was with some pleasure that I accepted an unusual, but very attractive invitation to LA two years later. A year or so after the British Equestrian Centre had been opened at Stoneleigh one morning, quite unexpectedly, an American turned up there, asking to see the centre manager, Charles Stratton. He wished to be shown everything, inside and out, as he was involved in the starting of such a centre in America. Obviously his centre was going to be very much more ambitious than Stoneleigh, involving a cross-country course and several dressage manèges. In fact it was part of a huge sports complex, also comprising expensive villas, about thirty miles from the centre of Los Angeles.

He seemed very impressed with all that he saw, even saying that he would like to sponsor one of the bars at Stoneleigh which he suggested should be known as the Diamond Bar, as Diamond Bar was the name of the area where he was opening his centre. It seemed most appropriate and we were very appreciative. A few weeks later Charles Stratton received a phone call from America. It was our American friend, extending an invitation for Charles Stratton, Colonel Bill Froud – the National Coach and the Centre's senior instructor – and myself to go out for the opening of Diamond Bar; furthermore, he would be delighted if I would perform the opening ceremony. The invitation, he intimated, included our wives. Despite the fact that it was for eight days only a week after the hunting season had started and despite the inability of Jennifer to accompany me as she would be running the Hunt Ball at Pendley that week, it was just too good an invitation to miss, especially as we would be flown out first-class and would be accommodated at the fabulous Beverley Hilton.

In due course two large Cadillacs met us at Los Angeles airport, which mercifully, that afternoon was free from smog. Having booked in at the hotel it was suggested that, after a rest, we should join our host at a little reception when we would be introduced to other personalities involved. Our contact who had visited Stoneleigh and invited us was one Don Macadam. He was under forty, but a millionaire,

although one felt that he could well lose a million as quickly as
he could make it – which it was later rumoured that he did. He
was very short, blonde and swarthy, with a good sense of
humour and tremendous energy. The President of Trans
World International, which apparently was promoting the
whole complex, was a charming Ralph Venner who was as tall
and slim as Don Macadam was short and thickset. After
generous dispensing of champagne we were each given a
magnificent wide leather belt with a decorated and embossed
buckle, each with our own name. We were then entertained to
a lavish dinner before retiring to our very welcome beds.

The following morning we were driven out to the Pomona
Valley where we saw for the first time this remarkable complex with its display houses, timber and stone with large
balconies and sun lounges, stretching up a rocky slope, an
eighteen-hole golf course, riding tracks, a partly completed
cross-country course and the great riding school, large enough
to contain an Olympic-size dressage arena, with magnificent
stabling and offices attached. In the background were the
mountains which in winter would become ski-ing slopes. We
could but be enormously impressed. If only our own National
Centre could be as magnificent as this; if only we could have
this kind of money behind us at Stoneleigh! On a beautiful day
it all looked wonderfully enticing, although, in fact, the whole
complex was far from complete and finishing touches were
still being carried out at the riding school complex for the
official opening three days hence.

Returning to Los Angeles we stopped at an inn for a steak
and beer, although it was between four and five o'clock; it was
my first experience of the fact that there are no regular meal
times amongst the business community in America. They
seem to eat just when it is convenient or possible – there is no
evidence of downing tools for a two-hour lunch break at one
o'clock, let alone 'everything stops for tea'. There was another
example that evening of what seemed to be a fairly common
practice amongst the American rich. While we were congre-
gating for dinner in the hotel vestibule we noticed a large
number of smartly dressed people, the ladies very bejewelled,
queuing to enter the ballroom where, it appeared, there was to
be a banquet for about 500 people. An elderly American lady,

friendly but obviously a little surprised at our informal dress, asked if we were going to the banquet. We told her that we were not but that we thought it looked a very grand occasion; presumably some charity function, we suggested. Oh yes, and the tickets were $300 each, she gushingly informed us. What was it in aid of, we asked? Surprisingly the lady had no idea, no idea at all; but it was going to be a grand party, Senator Blank was going to be there – such a pity that we were not going.

Next day a car was laid on to take us to Disneyland. Nothing that has ever been written about Disneyland is an exaggeration. It is unbelievable, an experience which must rank as one of the most remarkable in one's life. It so impressed me that I found myself thinking seriously of making the effort to bring my children out – they were then about 12 and 10 – especially to visit Disneyland. Fortunately when I returned home the euphoria had subsided, probably because by then I had realised just how much money it would actually entail. Nevertheless I am immensely grateful that I had the good fortune to spend a day at Disneyland, though really to benefit from it all one needed at least three days.

Rain fell almost ceaselessly during the day before the opening, culminating in a dramatic thunderstorm. In the early evening, news reached us at the hotel that out at Diamond Bar there was serious flooding. A young ex-patriot Englishman who appeared to act as Don Macadam's amanuensis told us that the opening was likely to be postponed, but that Don was out there master-minding a rescue operation. We were still unaware of exactly what the position was when we retired to bed at about midnight. However when we were breakfasting in the coffee shop next morning Don himself breezed in to tell us that all was well. The water rushing down the mountainside had forced a channel under the end walls of the new school and carried away all the tan and sand that had formed the surface of the arena. Acting as can only dynamic tycoons who are millionaires before they are thirty – and probably become bankrupt at thirty-five before they become millionaires again at forty – Don had organised the immediate delivery of a million tons of sand and tan to be put down through the night and the crevasses created by the torrential rain to be shored up. The opening would take place as near the advertised time as possible. We were greatly impressed. It would have been unfortunate if our journey had been in vain.

Some of our experiences during the next twenty-four hours can be described only as bizarre in the extreme; indeed, had I not been involved in them personally I would never have believed them. Not surprisingly everything both inside and outside the complex was still very wet when we arrived for the opening. Even the stable gangways, all part of the complex, were layers of wet mud, all of which, undoubtedly, was responsible for some of the strange things which were so to bedevil our efforts that afternoon. When we joined Ralph Venner in the President's Box, after our tour of the whole area to see what had miraculously been achieved, the rain had stopped but we were pretty damp, especially as far as our footwear was concerned. After a few words to the assembled company – about 500 people – from Ralph Venner, who spoke into one microphone, I was asked to make a short speech declaring the Diamond Bar Riding Area open, using a second microphone. I stepped forward, switched it on, but nothing happened. I looked round helplessly for an engineer but there was no one in sight. I switched on again. To my relief there was a loud click. I started to speak, but as I did so another voice dominated mine. I stopped, and listened. I could not believe my ears. It was unmistakably the voice of Richard Nixon, President of the United States. Had a message of goodwill from the President for Diamond Bar been specially recorded to be transmitted at the opening – I would not have put it beyond the ingenuity of Don Macadam, or the influence of Ralph Venner – without my being aware of it? But a few more words quickly showed that the President's speech was of purely political content, and nothing to do with Diamond Bar, or the party from England.

After a minute or so the voice was silenced. An engineer appeared, tinkered with my microphone for some minutes, then suggested that I try again. This time, to my relief, all was well. I duly made my little speech, thanked and congratulated the appropriate people, and declared the Centre officially open: Diamond Bar was in business. I never did hear a convincing explanation of what had happened or how something the President had been saying, presumably in Washington, had been picked up on an internal broadcast at Pomona. Indeed, it soon all became comparatively unimportant, thanks to this incident, strange enough in itself, being followed by one that was even more strange; while even this second incident was preceded by something which was not only strange but could, or so it seemed to me, have been serious, even fatal.

Immediately after the opening, Bill Froud, the British Horse Society's national coach, had been invited to take a clinic. He had a class of twelve or so but it had been arranged, in order to make it both more interesting and important, that I should be invited, as he proceeded with his class, to ask him, for the benefit of the large audience, to explain exactly what he was doing and what he was expecting from his pupils. In order to do this effectively I had asked if, in addition to Bill's radio mike, I could have a microphone at the edge of the ring. Not entirely to my surprise when I switched it on it did not work. The engineer came into the ring but even after he had taken it to pieces it still did not work. He suggested, therefore, that as we knew that the microphone in the President's Box was now working properly, and there was just sufficient lead, we should take that microphone from its stand and bring it down to the arena, where I could use it as a hand-mike. He hurried up to the gallery, dismantled the stand microphone, then to save time, so that it would not have be unplugged for him to bring it down, he tossed it down to me from the gallery. I caught it in one hand – and was flat on my back! I was standing on the sodden tan and my wet rubber-soled shoes obviously acted as a conductor, and an electric shock passed right through my body though, presumably due to the fact that I had rubber-soled shoes, not fatally. I rose to my feet considerably shaken. Not surprisingly, surely, I firmly refused to pick up the microphone as instructed by the engineer who, perhaps, thought that I had just drunk too much. At this incident there was, as can be imagined, considerable consterna tion: Bill Froud refused to start until his microphone had been properly tested, Ralph Venner insisted that the problems were fully sorted out before the clinic commenced. Eventually, after various comings and goings and the appearance of another engineer, it was decided that it was now completely

safe to proceed. I therefore briefly introduced Bill Froud as
Britain's National Coach, outlined his career and told the
audience something of what he would be attempting to
achieve in his clinic which was to be spread over two days. I
then handed over to him.

Switching on his microphone he began to speak, but he had
only spoken a few words when suddenly, mysteriously, his
voice was interrupted by mine. He signalled to me to stop
talking as he had now taken over from me. But I was *not*
speaking – I had not said a word; yet coming out of the
loudspeakers all round the school was my voice, loud and
clear. What was more, it appeared that I was giving a lecture,
some sort of instruction. In fact, obviously I was talking about
stable-management, the right utensils, the correct bedding.
My voice was completely dominating Bill's. Putting his hand
over his microphone he called across to me, in so many words
suggesting that I should belt up.

'I'm sorry', I called back, 'but I'm not speaking.'

'Then, who the hell's voice is it?'

There could be no doubt but that it was mine; I could not
deny it. What was more, as I listened there seemed to be
something increasingly familiar about what I was saying.
Stable utensils, proper bedding . . . It rang a bell. Of course!
That record!

'For goodness sake turn the thing off', Bill yelled. 'This is
impossible.'

I called across to the engineer to take down the radio
microphone and carried my stand mike across to the centre of
the arena where Bill was sitting on the horse that had been
provided for him. By holding the mike up to him I enabled
him to repeat his opening remarks – uninterrupted. As can be
imagined we were extremely embarrassed as to the audience it
really did look as though we were both trying to give
instruction at the same time, yet my own conscience was clear.
Once I had introduced Bill I had said absolutely nothing. We
managed to get through that brief opening session without
any further hitches – indeed what else *could* happen? – though it
was not easy when Bill asked his class to ride round the outside
of the arena as they had to cross the microphone lead which
stretched from the edge to the centre. Having seen what had

happened to me earlier the riders were, not surprisingly, somewhat apprehensive; but they all survived.

The mystery was never wholly cleared up, although one of the Centre's staff did recall that a series entitled 'Horse and Pony Management' – the record that I had originally recorded for Quartilles International Ltd – had been being transmitted on one of the many different radio programmes in the west. Somehow, due to the freak conditions which had first of all produced the voice of the American President, then floored me, the somewhat dodgy system had finally picked up my talk which was being broadcast at that precise moment on another wavelength for another programme. The story later circulated that my voice was actually coming from another country altogether: Canada or Mexico or the West Indies. I have no idea. I was prepared to believe anything. I only know that I never received any royalties!

It had been bad enough my Richard III being interrupted by my commentary on the Olympic Games at a small village fête in 1948. It was far worse that twenty years later my voice should be interrupting the first clinic at the prestigious opening of the new equestrian centre at Diamond Bar in California. 'Do you never stop talking?' was the cynical comment of one of our party.

The weekend saw the first big show jumping at Diamond Bar. Apart from Barbara Simpson from Canada who rode her own horse Australis, the invited riders were mounted on horses kindly provided by members of the American Federation. Anneli Drummond Hay was loaned an attractive, but inexperienced, grey five-year-old called Harlequin. The main event was the Grand Prix on the Sunday afternoon. Don Macadam seemed determined that Anneli should win it though the hot favourite was Barbara Simpson. Nor was there any shortage of really good American riders. There was even a suggestion that Don had somehow fiddled matters to ensure that Anneli qualified, but if he did – and I certainly cannot think how he did it – nobody seemed to mind. Anneli had endeared herself to the audience and if somehow Don could so manipulate it that she appeared in the final, well – so be it! I have no doubt that it was all above board, just as I have no doubt that he had fallen for Anneli, making no effort to conceal it. Everybody knew about it so, doubtless, there were some who liked to think that he had somehow 'waggoned' it. He certainly could not in any way have influenced the final jump-off against the clock, which Anneli won, in a real thriller demonstrating to the American crowd her exceptional ability at its most brilliant. I had, over the years, seen Anneli win many top-class competitions from the three-day event at Badminton to the Queen Elizabeth Cup at the Royal International – and the Olgiata in Rome; but I never saw her ride more effectively than that afternoon. Nor have I witnessed anything more impressive than the way in which, in two days, she improved this green novice into an extremely able top-class show jumper. Rumour had it that behind the scenes either Anneli or Alan Oliver, who was also competing – and distinguishing himself – tried to buy Harlequin, but I never heard what exactly happened to this singularly attractive young horse with so much potential. It must surely have been a winner for somebody.

I had originally been invited to do the public address commentary on this event, but as a result of a strange experience – yet another! – that I had had at the show the previous day I decided not to. From the very day that I had first been invited to Los Angeles it had been implied that I would be expected to do some commentating; indeed, that I might well be expected to do some television. The television never materialised, but on the first day of the show the Centre Manager asked if I would be prepared to take over the public address for the major event the following day. Naturally I was happy to agree, providing, of course, that the regular commentator did not object, which I was assured was most unlikely. When I arrived at Diamond Bar shortly before the competition was due to start I reported at the commentary box. The regular commentator was already there and made no effort to vacate his position. Neither Don Macadam nor the Centre Manager were in evidence so I felt it best just to wait until I was invited to take over. When it was time for the competition to start the regular commentator announced it and, immediately the first horse entered the arena, began his commentary. It was only then that the Centre Manager, presumably hearing not my voice but their regular commentator's, came up and asked me to take over. The regular commentator looked extremely displeased but eventually made way for me, just leaving me with the microphone, not even introducing me. Somewhat embarrassed I settled down to the job. I had taken the trouble to do my homework, so was well enough informed about the competitors, being able, of course, really to expand on the few that I knew from the European international circuit; but not speaking, as is the American custom, actually during a round.

It seemed to go quite well, everyone later making kind remarks about my English style of commentary. Without a word the regular commentator took my place for the next competition, and I made myself scarce. Back at the hotel that evening I was formally invited to cover the Grand Prix the next afternoon. Fortunately I was able to say that I had been invited to commentate on the radio and, therefore, would find it difficult to do the public address as well. In fact, not speaking on the public address during a round, I could easily have done both, or just agreed to do either one or the other for the jump-off; but it was, of course, the obvious disapproval of the regular commentator that made me unwilling to take his place again. It was only after the show was over that Charles Stratton discovered what the real trouble was. The regular commentator assumed that if I did his job I would also be taking his fee. Such a thing had never for one moment occurred to me. I was a guest who had received wonderful hospitality; the very least that I could do was to help in any way that I could – if nothing else, it helped to repay the cost of bringing me out from England. What I did not realise, of course, was that the regular commentator received a fee of $800, then about £500, for each day's commentating. At that time, in England, I received £25 or £30 a day for a public address commentary! No wonder he resented my being invited to do the job. I only wish that I had been able to reassure him; but it must have been a nice surprise for him when he received his full fee, and perhaps he felt a little guilty at the way he had behaved towards a fellow commentator.

Our visit was nearly at its end. On the last day Don Macadam drove us out to his beautiful estate, or ranch, in South California. We gathered that he and his wife had married as childhood sweethearts, but were now in the process of leaving each other, which lent a rather moving sadness to the beauty of the place in the early fall. That evening he entertained us to drinks in his fabulous down-town flat before taking us out to dinner. Back in his flat after dinner he insisted on presenting Anneli with a magnificent fur coat. Rumour had it that she finished up with two. He certainly seemed in the mood to give her the world. There were all sorts of rumours and raised eyebrows when next morning she did not turn up at the airport. But we need not have worried. Anneli is adept at missing planes and arrived home safely a day later.

What happened to Don I have no idea. He appeared once in England a year or two later, by which time he seemed to have severed his connection with Trans Continental. Rumour had it that he went bankrupt, but I doubt if we need worry about him too much. He was a born survivor, as well as excellent company; and he certainly provided me with a memorable trip to LA.

Chapter 8

Blue Blood – For a Fat Fee

France

For some years the BBC has run a highly thought-of 'occasional' series called 'Horizon'. I was interested to hear that they were going to do a series on the thoroughbred. I was, naturally, very pleased to be invited by the producer, Christopher Lafontaine, to take part. He wanted me to accompany him to a well known French stud and the famous equestrian centre at Saumur. It sounded a most attractive assignment, the only snag being that it was the first week of my twenty-sixth and last season as Master of the Whaddon Chase. I had never liked missing a day's hunting when I was Master; not only because I was missing the sport, but equally because I felt that, as Master, it was my responsibility to be out. There are always decisions to be taken, problems to be resolved. For the first fifteen years of my Mastership, before I had a joint-Master, I used to persuade the BBC to include a clause in my contract to the effect that I could not be made to accept a Saturday job between 1 November and 31 March; and in those fifteen years I doubt if I missed half a dozen days. This 'Horizon' programme in November 1979 particularly appealed to me, so I happily agreed to do it as it was worked out that it would be quite possible for me to hunt on Tuesday, catch an early flight to Paris, on Wednesday, returning early on Saturday morning in time for hunting on Saturday. In any event, I had a most competent deputy in Peter Stoddart.

That season a friend had lent me a very attractive exsteeplechaser called Brough, which had won some useful races, and to which I had taken quite a fancy. He was a beautiful ride, very fast, and jumped in a spectacular fashion – except just occasionally over timber when, like so many

steeplechasers, he would take a liberty jumping off his fore-
hand, instead of off his hocks, expecting to be able to go
through the top as on a racecourse. At the very end of this day
in November Brough did just this, over a gate. As we were
going fast, breasting the gate he turned a complete somersault;
that was bad enough, but as he struggled to his feet he played
football with me. It was some moments before I could rise to
my feet while I assessed how many bones were broken.
Fortunately there appeared to be no serious damage apart, as it
was later discovered, from two cracked ribs. Before the end of
the evening, however, I was black and blue all over and very
stiff. The prospects for my journey the following morning
were not propitious. I had to drive to Heathrow, fly to Paris,
take a coach to the station, train to Le Mans, and finally was to
be driven by Christopher Lafontaine to Mesnil.

Well aware that television producers and their like tend to
think it mildly eccentric to set such store on a day's hunting I
was determined, if I could, to conceal my problems from
Christopher, disguising as best I could my limp, refraining
from wincing when he bumped into me, pulling my sleeve
down as far as possible to conceal my bruised and swollen
wrist and sitting down as naturally as I could manage, rather
than easing myself into my seat, which would have been very
much more comfortable. I succeeded for a little more than
twelve hours.

Christopher met me at Le Mans and took me to a café
opposite the station, as we were not expected at Mesnil until
six o'clock. Though never considering myself a motor-racing
enthusiast, apart from some exciting afternoons as a boy at
Brooklands – where I actually saw Sir Malcolm Campbell –
there was something intriguing in finding myself at Le Mans,
for so long associated with the great twenty-four-hour race.
Actually to drive along some of the roads used by many of the
most famous racing drivers in motor-racing history was an
experience that I enjoyed enormously, determining me one
day to see the race for myself; needless to say I never have.

It was not a long drive to Mesnil, fortunately for me, but I
would happily have driven ten times as far had I known the
pleasures that were awaiting me. Mesnil was in many ways a
typical French château, but, being white and in no way

sombre or oppressive, it was much more elegant than many French châteaux. Bathed in the evening sun it looked mellow and friendly, and encouragingly welcoming: arriving at a place where one knows, or is known, to nobody can be daunting. There proved to be nothing daunting about Mesnil: far from it.

Haras du Mesnil belonged to a quite remarkable old lady, Madame Elizabeth Couturié. To all intents and purposes she was French – no one would ever have thought otherwise; indeed, she seemed the personification of the French grande dâme of a château, the châtelaine. In fact, she was American. She had been educated in England, where she still had many friends, but in the First World War she had been taken to America, living for the remainder of the War in California where she met the man whom she was later to marry, and returned to France with him to set up the famous stud. He died in the sixties, but she continued to run the stud, possessing, obviously, great knowledge and expertise. She was now seventy-seven.

Some expert in the racing world had recommended Le Mesnil to Christopher Lafontaine for his 'Horizon' programme. When he visited her to make arrangements he mentioned that I would be with him, whereupon she insisted that we should stay at the château as she believed that we had mutual friends; at any rate she had recently read one of my books, still being very involved in all things English. She was small, but very active, and extremely easy to talk to. We were first offered a glass of white wine in a large, slightly gloomy salon, obviously welcomingly cool in summer, but typically French with its massive oak furniture and heavy brocade curtains; and then we were shown to our rooms. Mine was spacious, with a large bathroom and wide windows facing south and west, looking out over the charming gardens. On a table was a tray with a bottle of whisky and a glass.

'Englishmen always like whisky before dinner,' she said, 'so just help yourself.'

Whether Chris had one in his room I did not discover, but I was certainly ready for mine, as I was for the very hot and soothing bath in which I wallowed for some twenty minutes.

As I sat next to her at dinner she began to tell me something of her earlier life, which was certainly romantic, especially when it came to the years of the occupation. But nothing could have been more romantic than the story that unfolded during the next morning of Right Royal V, the most famous product of Le Mesnil – indeed, one of the most famous French stallions of the century.

The well known American breeder of thoroughbreds John Widener, who was a great friend of the Couturiés, decided when, in 1945, he was in failing health that he would take all the horses that he owned in France back to Kentucky, with just two exceptions. One of these was an old mare by Ksar called Barberybush; he doubted that she would survive the journey by sea to America. As he could never have brought himself either to sell her or have her put down he offered her to the Couturiés as a token of his friendship. The following year the old mare produced a filly foal, her last, but they were never sure whether it was by Tornado or Victrix. Appropriately – or so it seemed to me – they called her Bastia. She was not easy to train and very small, as a result of which she was never raced. In any event racing in France, in the aftermath of the War, was going through a very difficult time and there was no point putting horses into training unnecessarily. Madame Couturié, however, had been keen for some time to introduce Hyperion blood into her stud as it was then non-existent in France. She therefore decided shortly after the War to send Bastia to Owen Tudor in England. Oddly enough although he had won the Derby as a three-year-old and the Ascot Gold Cup the following year it was not difficult to get a nomination at a reasonable figure.

The following year Madame Couturié was approached by a British bloodstock agent who asked if she was prepared to sell any mares to England. Trade in France still being very poor at that time she was easily persuaded to sell Bastia. Minutes before the in-foal mare was due to leave for England her stud groom informed her that Bastia had started to foal, early. As soon as she saw the foal she knew that it was something special. In less than an hour she had phoned England and cancelled the sale. She called the foal Right Royal V. It grew well, becoming more impressive at each phase of its development. At eighteen months, already standing over sixteen hands, it was sent to one of the most successful trainers in France at that time, Etienne Pollet, who was equally impressed. As a two-year-old Right Royal won his first four races on the trot, was then beaten into second, when it was later discovered that he was running a temperature, and was not beaten again that season. As a three-year-old he just failed to win his first race having, according to his owner, been left far too much to do, 'although I hate making excuses'. He was never again defeated until, very unluckily in the opinion of most racegoers, he went down by a short head to Molvedo in the Prix de l'Arc de Triomphe. Previously in the Prix de Jockey Club and in the Prix Lupin, he had beaten Match, which as a four-year-old won both the King George VI and Queen Elizabeth Stakes and the Laurel International. In 1961 Right Royal was himself to win the King George VI and Queen Elizabeth Stakes, beating by no less than six lengths St Paddy. He was ridden as usual on that occasion by Roger Poincelet in the famous black and white diamond colours, which thus became as famous in England as in France.

At stud Right Royal sired over twenty horses that won classics or Group I races. He was probably at the very height of his stud career when in 1973 he died. There were tears in Madame Couturié's eyes as she told me, standing by his grave under the trees in the little orchard at Le Mesnil, how one day he had playfully reared up, lost his balance, crashed over backwards, breaking a leg. I never saw Right Royal himself, of course, but was greatly impressed by a two-year-old grandson, very dark bay with just two white socks on his hind legs. Christopher Lafontaine's cameras achieved some wonderful pictures of this young stallion; but it was when he wanted to take a shot with me standing by his head, my right hand on his poll, speaking straight to the camera, as he nuzzled the sugar in my left hand, that I had to admit to being unable to lift my right arm high enough, thanks to my badly bruised shoulder. The truth was out; after which Christopher was very solicitous of my comfort even if he was thinking how foolish hunting people must be.

Madame Couturié was very proud that our Queen had sent a mare to Right Royal; even prouder that she had paid a brief visit to France to visit the Rothschild stud next door and Le

Mesnil itself, where Madame Couturié had entertained her to
lunch. 'Your Queen', she told me, 'is a very remarkable
person: she knows even more about thoroughbreds than I do.'

How proud she must have been when shortly before she
died Golden Fleece won the Derby! To replace Right Royal
she had acquired Northern Treat by Northern Dancer out of
Exotic Treat by Vaguely Noble. Golden Fleece, by Nijinsky,
was also out of Exotic Treat, so Le Mesnil was right back on
the map. It is now run by Madame Couturié's grandson, who
is married to the daughter of Frank Feeney, owner of the
Ardoon Stud in County Kildare. I have never considered
myself a racing man, but I have always looked upon my visit
to Le Mesnil as one of the highlights of my equestrian life. The
weather was glorious with the early autumn sunlight and
colours; the setting unforgettable; the company so charming.
To have met Madame Couturié was a privilege. I was sad that
it had never been possible to accept her invitation to take
Jennifer over for a few days.

Saumur
Next morning we drove to Saumur, not taking the direct
route, so that we could enjoy to the full the Loire Valley with
all its charming little villages, its farms and châteaux. Our
hotel at Saumur was just by the bridge within walking
distance of the old Cavalry School buildings and riding hall in
the centre of the town. When originally, at Christopher's
request, I had approached the authorities at Saumur for
filming facilities I encountered considerable resistance.
Indeed, we seemed to be getting nowhere, until I asked Jack
Reynolds, then Secretary General of the British Equestrian
Federation, to contact on my behalf his opposite number in
France. The reaction was very different. On our arrival we
were entertained with champagne by the Commandant and
his aides. One of his staff was instructed to provide us with
anything that we might require. We were given maps and
brochures. We had hoped, we said, to see a display of Le Cadre
Noir, but had been informed that the Cadre only gave its
display on Sundays; we had wanted to film the magnificent
new stable block which housed 250 horses but had been told
that for security reasons this was not open to the public; we

had wanted to get some action shots on the spacious cross-country training areas with its three courses, but no students were in residence. The personal contact, however, produced miracles. Three of the staff had been instructed to meet us up at the cross-country course that afternoon. We could film where we liked at the stables. The Cadre Noir was to put on a special display at 8.30 a.m. next morning.

We tackled the stable area first, which took us about two hours. This meant that we were late arriving at the cross-country course, but those waiting for us did not seem in the least resentful. It took Chris half an hour or so to select a suitable area, the end of a leafy ride with a set of rails about fifty yards from the end and imposing parallels over a wide ditch at the very end, where it came out into open country. First there had to be a 'scene set', but this entailed difficulties as it involved my climbing a fence, which I was quite incapable of doing; eventually Christopher settled for a close-up of my head and shoulders with cut-away shots to the various features on the course. Finally we were ready for the shots of three riders galloping through the wood and over the fences, with commentary from myself. The first rider approached, over the rails in the ride, then: 'Coming now to the parallels – my God!' I have seldom seen a more crashing fall. Hitting the first pole the horse turned a complete somersault landing on top of its rider. Such was the force that the girth snapped clean in half, the saddle landing some ten yards away.

Recalling my own experience two days earlier I was full of sympathy for the rider, but his senior officer merely called for a different saddle and told him to do it again. To my relief the horse refused: but we had got a marvellous 'action' shot, even if my original commentary had to be replaced with one that I dubbed on later.

It was not difficult to find a charming little restaurant that evening where we could relax and enjoy French cooking at its best. We went to bed contented, pleased with what we had achieved, looking forward to the next day and our session with the Cadre Noir. The effect of the excellent cognac on my battered body ensured a comfortable night. Next morning, however, I awoke with anxiety. A thick mist was lying on the river and swirling round the old town's narrow streets. Over

our coffee and croissants in the intimate panelled salon we
realised that there was little likelihood of our being able to film
at 8.30 a.m.

Right in the centre of the town there is a sanded manège in
front of the old Ecole de Cavalière, a magnificent backdrop.
Here each Sunday morning the Cadre Noir give their display
for the public. Now they were prepared to put on a special
display for us this Friday morning. When we arrived at the site
it was covered in heavy mist, almost a fog; but the full
complement of the display, both those who do the individual
exercises – similar to the Spanish Riding School of Vienna,
levade, courbette, capriole – known as the sauteurs, and the
quadrille, were already present. Like ghosts they appeared
from and disappeared into the mist, silently, their movements
muffled by the sand and the encompassing fog. After an hour
it seemed to lighten a little. It was suggested that they might
commence part of their performance to see if it were possible
from a camera point of view. Alas, it was not. Christopher had
anticipated brilliant early morning sunshine. It was suggested
that the old Cavalry School, now completely refurbished,
might be used; but the lighting was inadequate.

As we returned to the manège the sun was beginning to
peep through. Surely the mist would be gone in a few minutes;
but it persisted. It produced, however, an effect of unbelievable beauty. The mist, now rose, swirled, floated along the
ground. Moving in it, all the horses were entirely visible
except their legs below the knees. It could only be described as
ethereal. Hurriedly Christopher summoned his cameras.
Briskly the *Ecuyer en Chef* called up the Cadre to commence its
display. It was a breathtaking performance. The horses
appeared to float through their movements, suddenly rising in
their levades or courbettes as they might from the sea.
Christopher was excited beyond description. I was speechless;
the exquisite beauty spoke for itself, made all the lovelier by
the quality of the horses – all French thoroughbreds – so much
more attractive, more active than the Lippizaners, even if not
so accurate or, in the exercises, so athletic.

The policy of the French Government over the last two or
three decades to invest heavily in a breeding policy has paid
very real dividends. There are now some twenty-four national

studs, producing not only thoroughbreds, but heavy horses as well. The result is that the French Federation is able to insist that no rider may represent France in a national team other than on a French-bred horse. Just as since the War the strength of the Germans lies in their ability to provide an endless supply of Hanovarians and to a lesser extent Trakheners, West-phalians, Holsteiners, France increasingly is finding itself in a similar position which must, in part, be responsible for their recent international successes.

Would that Britain could find itself equally fortunate; but the equivalent of £8 million that the French Government spends on equestrianism compared with the £100,000 pro-vided by the British Sports Council on behalf of the British Government tells its own story. Nor does there seem any likelihood of any British Government becoming more generous.

Obviously it is not difficult to criticise individually the horses used by the Cadre Noir. If they were top-class thoroughbreds they would be on the racecourse; if they were a little less than top class they would be eventing or jumping. They are nevertheless elegant, full of quality, beautifully turned out, with the result that even without the sun-tipped ground-mist swirling round their feet and fetlocks they gave immense aesthetic pleasure. It was certainly a memorable morning at Saumur, rounded off with a glass of champagne with the senior officers in the old riding school where I was invited to sign their historic visitors' book. It was only sad that when eventually the finished product was shown on BBC 2 scarcely two minutes of all the time spent in Saumur were included, even less of Le Mesnil. But that, regretfully, is television. Is it surprising that programmes are so costly to produce or that the BBC is short of money?

As a result of the delay we were much later setting off for Paris than we had intended. Worse, the mist that had been lying around all morning had become dense fog by mid-afternoon. I was thankful not to be driving, and even more thankful when, after several times losing our way in the outskirts of Paris, Christopher had found his way to the little pension which he was sure would accommodate us. Effi-ciently, before leaving Saumur he had managed to transfer our

flights from the late evening on the Friday to the 11.00 a.m.
plane on the Saturday morning. It meant missing the hunting,
that I had so carefully planned, of course, but perhaps it was as
well in view of the stiffness and soreness that I was still
experiencing, especially after a six-hour drive in Christopher's
hired mini.

It was even foggier next morning when, Christopher having completed the endless telephone calls that seem to be
inescapable from any producer's responsibilities, we set off for
the airport – the fog, incidentally, making the extraordinary
Pompidou building, as we passed it, look even more
grotesque than it is. We arrived at the airport, having again
twice lost our way, at exactly the time that the plane was about
to leave. It seemed obvious to me, however, that no plane
could fly in this fog, so I was not particularly agitated. In fact,
to my astonishment, while Christopher was still handing over
his hired car, half a mile away, our flight was called. There was
nothing for it but for me to leave without him – but just as the
plane doors were being closed a tall, tousled, breathless figure
burst in. Christopher had made it. We landed, alarmingly, in
thick fog at Heathrow, but only fifteen minutes late. I find it
difficult to believe that we were not on automatic control,
though officially it had not then been introduced. Jennifer was
there waiting for me. The meet, she informed me, had been
cancelled, so I had missed nothing; but I had had an unforgettable three days in Le Loire enjoying to the full the French
thoroughbred at two levels of its excellence.

Pompadour
I was fortunate enough a year or two later to visit one of the
National Studs at Pompadour, probably the second largest
stud in France (the largest being Haras du Pins). It is
immensely impressive, based at the famous château in
Limousin. The château itself is used for administration.
Across the road are the magnificent stable blocks housing
no less than fifty-two stallions: every sort of horse
from thoroughbred and Arab to Percheron and Welsh.
Unfortunately most of the Percherons are bred for meat, but
were it not for this – to the British way of thinking – somewhat
unpalatable fact, there would be no Percherons at all: few of

9a. Debbie Johnsey on Moxy, first to go in the delayed jump-off at Bromont. Inexperience, perhaps, affected her 'touch' in such terrible conditions, and she was narrowly defeated for the bronze medal.

9b. The tricky 'slalom' on the three-day-event cross-country course at Bromont. It involved four sharp turns through the trees. Princess Anne, despite the size and strength of Goodwill, owned by the Queen, went through brilliantly.

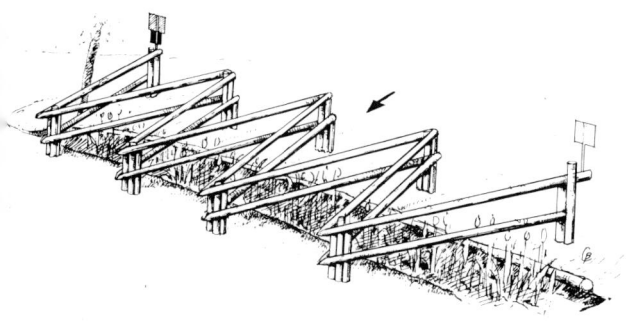

9c. The 'pony club' fence at Bromont, which I never even bothered to measure, but which caused Princess Anne's downfall. She took off on the extreme right, as instructed, but, thanks to torrential overnight rain, this had become a bog.

10a. The Exhibition of the Advanced Economic Achievements in the Ukranian Socialist Soviet Republic – the venue for the European Three-Day Event Championships at Kiev in 1973. The individual British competitor, Rosalyn Jones, does her dressage in front of its main feature.

10b. The individual winner, Alex Evdokimov on Jeger, receives his trophy from Prince Philip, President of the International Federation.

11a. Goodwill, ridden by Princess Anne, having taken off a full stride too soon at the horror Fence 2 at Kiev, just fails to clear the far pole with his hind legs . . .

11b. . . . giving Princess Anne a crashing fall on to the rock-hard ground, after which she retired.

12a. Another Fence 2 casualty, Bengtsson from Sweden on Iller.

12b. Janet Hodgson, spattered with blood after her own fall at Fence 2, carries on on Larkspur to ensure the survival of the British team, which eventually won the silver medal.

13a. Colonel 'Babe' Moseley in Moscow: 'Second-class tourists! We have two representatives of the BBC with us!'

13b. Bruce Davidson on Might Tango stands well back at the Old Fort, a fence that caused much grief in the World Three-Day Event Championships in Lexington in 1978. He won the individual gold medal.

14a. The château that towers above the Loire, making Saumur one of the most romantic sites for any centre of equitation.

14b. The Cadre Noir on their French thoroughbreds rehearsing their display right in the town centre, in front of the old Cavalry School of Saumur.

15a. A well-filled mare and foal class in one of the small outside rings at the Royal Dublin Society's Show at Ballsbridge.

15b. For many, the most tense moment of the show at Dublin: the final judging for the supreme championship in the Jumping Enclosure.

16a. (*above left*) With me is Professor Ron Cole, enthusiastic organiser of the Equine Symposium at Calgary University.

16b. (*above right*) Hunter judges invited to officiate at the Royal Winter Fair in Toronto: myself with Pamela Arthur, eminent judge in Canada and America for twenty years, and Michael Page, individual bronze medallist in the Olympic Three-Day Event in 1968 and one of the judges most in demand in America: top hat, white tie and tails!

16c. Riding a four-year-old in the class for young stallions under saddle at Karstrup in Denmark. This compact chestnut finished second, only beaten by its full brother – which at least showed that the judging was consistent!

them are used on the farm today. Mares are sent to the stallions, and only occasionally does a stallion visit a mare. There is on average one groom to every three stallions. They are well quartered and well paid; there is, apparently, no shortage of applicants – all male – for jobs at Pompadour or, presumably, at the other studs. For the most part the daily exercising is done in pulling carriages, and only a few stallions are ridden, in a sand manège; others are led out.

Interestingly the stud acts as the organising agency for the whole area. A riding school, for instance, can operate only under a licence from the stud, which is involved in the appointment of the chief instructor who has to be Saumur-trained. It is not possible to ride more or less anywhere – on private land, bridle paths, moorland, woodlands and so on – as for the most part it is still in England; in France, individuals receive permits to ride in specific areas, usually as an organised party.

One very much has a feeling of money being no object; everything is beautifully maintained and highly organised, rather like a top-class racing stable in England. When I asked M de Pechdo, the Director of Pompadour, why it was that the French Government, even a Socialist Government, was prepared to spend so much money on equestrianism, he replied that apart from the fact that the breeding of the French thoroughbred was regarded as a sound investment, the Government believed that riding was a recreation and activity that should be enjoyed at all levels of society, just as much as tennis or golf. It was not their wish that it should be regarded as exclusive, as in Italy. I was greatly relieved that he did not say 'as in Britain', for whereas it is estimated that something approaching two million people ride in Britain, only a quarter of a million people ride in France.

About a mile away from the stud there is another complex which is the home for about sixty mares. I did not have the opportunity to see this, but, although a separate unit, it appeared to be complementary to the stud and is, of course, Government-financed. Less than a mile further on is one of the celebrated Clubs Mediteranées. This proved to be a real eye-opener. The Clubs Mediteranées are moderately priced holiday complexes with the emphasis very much on sport. At

the Pompadour Club Mediteranée amenities for only two
sports are provided: tennis and riding. There are no less than
nineteen covered tennis courts, with four hard courts outside.
As far as riding is concerned, seventy horses are kept permanently, an extra fifty being brought in at peak holiday time. Of
the three indoor riding schools two are of Olympic propor-
tions. There are eight *carrières*, outside *manèges* and riding
areas. There are also two cross-country courses, one for the
less experienced, one for the more advanced. An additional
one is being constructed with facilities for top-class riders.
There are eight full-time instructors, including a senior
Saumur-trained *écuyer*, and a young rider who a few years ago
won the Junior European Three-Day Event Championship.
There is instruction at some eight levels from what is referred
to as the Pony Club, riders between eight and twelve years,
right up to *l'Etrier d'Argent*, the silver medal level, approximately similar to the British Horse Society's senior instructor. In all there are about 200 acres surrounding the Club
where guests can ride or go for walks.

For young people it certainly makes an ideal holiday,
costing approximately £200 a week, inclusive of absolutely
everything; but the riders, about 40 per cent of the total 200
guests, pay a £50 surcharge, though this is waived if the
student bringing his own horse allows others to ride it. The
accommodation is in rooms for two, or for three, to ensure
that no one is ever left on his or her own. The food is generous
in the extreme. There is the usual continental breakfast, a help-
yourself lunch with about eight different serving tables,
groaning with both hot dishes and cold from which to choose;
and a four-course sit-down dinner at night. Wine is served free
at each meal. Not surprisingly the Pompadour Club
Mediteranée is booked in the holiday months three years
ahead. Even in off-season periods it is always full.

The Club Mediteranée is, of course, private enterprise. All
over the world there are some 150 Clubs, the majority of them
in Europe. The one at Quarzazate in Morocco is the only other
one that concentrates on riding, although riding is available at
many other Clubs. It would seem that the whole movement, if
it can be thus described, is very successful financially. Nevertheless, as far as the equestrianism is concerned, this does not

prevent the Government from being involved. For every French-bred horse bought for the centre – they are all purchased as three-year-olds by Colonel Guyon, who won the Three-Day Event Gold Medal in the Mexico Olympic Games – the Government provides all the keep for them until they are introduced into work at five or six years old; this amounts to about £3,000 per horse.

France is a country that has not usually been particularly associated with equestrianism – though surprisingly people tend to forget such successes as the show jumping team gold medal in 1976, Montreal, and the individual three-day event gold medal in Mexico, 1968, Pierre d'Oriola's two individual show jumping gold medals in Helsinki, 1952, and Tokyo, 1964, and his World Championship in Buenos Aires, 1966, Janou Lefèbvre's Women's World Championships in 1970 and 1974 and her European Championship in 1966 – no mean success. One can only congratulate the French Government on the generous, far-sighted attitude that it has taken towards equestrian activities – and hope to contain one's envy. There can be no doubt, however, that there must be many who envied *me* enjoying these very special occasions – and being paid a fat fee for the privilege.

Part III

An English Judge Overseas

Chapter 9

Beginnings

The first horse show at which I was invited to judge was East Grinstead in 1952. My co-judge was Colonel Neil Foster, my joint-Master in the Grafton Hunt. Mrs Gregson – a celebrated personality in the hunting world – told us quite blatantly that she was inviting us only as we were Masters of Fox Hounds and therefore should know what we were looking for in buying horses for the Hunt staff. Neil Foster had not much more experience than I in judging at that time, but I had always admired him both for his horsemanship and his eye for a horse.

The first class that we had to judge was for heavyweight hunters. Having seen them walk, trot and canter we lined them up in a provisional order with a big but rather common grey in fourth place. We were about to ride them when in stentorian tones a voice called out from the ringside: 'D'you know that horse you've put fourth is mine? Never been beaten.'

We both recognised the voice as belonging to a very wealthy man who with his new-found wealth had become a great patron of showing, particularly the hunter classes. He certainly had some very good horses, but this was not one of them, though it had apparently won a number of times as judges were a little inclined to put up anything belonging to this owner once they had recognised his regular rider. When we had finished riding them we had them stripped and run up.

'We'll teach that b— a lesson all right', said Neil. 'If we drop him a couple of places he won't even get a rosette.' So we brought him in sixth out of eight.

'Take him out!' yelled the owner to his rider, 'Take him out!', which he did.

As we left the ring a friend, well known in showing circles, accosted us and, laughing, assured us that we would never be invited to judge at another show, such was the influence of this wealthy patron. I had no doubt that he was right.

Fortunately, however, Captain Jack Webber, the long-respected Secretary General of the British Show Jumping Association, having been asked to organise a horse show for the Brighton Corporation, kindly invited me to judge. I accepted with some diffidence as, like East Grinstead, Brighton was in Sussex, the home of the wealthy patron. Not surprisingly he did not enter any of his horses, but ultimately Brighton was, I have always thought, a show which was to have a considerable influence on my career as a judge. In the preliminary judging of the middleweight class I called in first an exceptionally nice-looking brown horse, but which, when I rode it, I was convinced made a noise. Accordingly I informed the rider – one of the best known in showing – of my opinion and told her that if she stayed in I could only put her down. To my surprise when it came to the final judging in the afternoon she returned, handing me a vet's certificate as she rode past me. Quickly looking at it I realised that the signature was one of the Show's official veterinary surgeons'. Obviously, therefore, I could not turn it out; but I decided to put it only third to ensure that it would not come into the Championship. One day the following season I noticed this horse out hunting with the Grafton ridden by a visitor. Not at all to my surprise it was obviously a brilliant horse, which made me feel that I had made a fool of myself spinning it. A year later, however, the visitor came out again, but on a different horse. On enquiring what had happened to the brown horse I was informed that it had – yes, gone in the wind! It had always made a noise, I was informed by the rider, who was not the professional who had ridden it at Brighton, so I felt that my action had been justified.

My working hunter class at Brighton that year consisted of about fifteen horses all of which were very much of a muchness. When I rode them, therefore, I decided at the end of each ride to jump one of the fences. At least this helped me to make up my mind, for in a working hunter class it was surely a good jumper that I was looking for. I certainly was not aware that any of the riders objected to my action although I appreciated that it might be considered a little unconventional. Later, however, I learned that there had been a number of complaints. Supposing I had had a fall and damaged a horse; supposing due to my own inefficiency a horse had refused, having jumped perfectly for its owner; supposing one of the horses had knocked a fence down (though, in fact, none of them either refused or hit a fence)? Was it not against the rules? Not specifically, simply because at that time there were very few rules for the Hunter Improvement Society's panel of judges. It was, however, unusual behaviour for a judge and I had little doubt that invitations to judge in the future would be few and far between.

Surprisingly it proved to be exactly the opposite. Brighton, apparently earned me a reputation for independence – I should like to think integrity – with the result that for the next several years I was invited to judge at about thirty shows each year. Most remarkable of all, when the wealthy patron from Sussex retired his outstanding champion he very kindly offered to give it to me as a hunter – an offer that sadly I had to refuse as I just had not room in my yard for another hunter, and those that I had at that time were all too good to replace. Another Master of Hounds was fortunate enough to acquire this great horse and had many good seasons on it, actually hunting hounds.

Dublin

Although in the mid-fifties I was doing plenty of judging, at important shows as well as at the smaller ones, I was delighted when at the International at the White City in July 1955, only two or three years after I had started judging, I was invited by that great character Judge Wylie, who for so many years had run the Royal Dublin Society's Show at Ballsbridge, to judge at Dublin in 1955. The old Judge, who also, in his own inimitable style, did all the public address commentaries on the jumping events at Dublin, which was, perhaps, what interested him in me, was quite frank in admitting, that he was only asking me as my father who had judged at Dublin for twenty-five consecutive years was retiring as a judge; it would be nice, he thought, if his son carried on, which I did until

1980, though after the Judge's death fresh judges were, rightly, introduced with the result that one used to be invited only every two or three years rather than every year. Nevertheless, my father and I between us spanned some fifty years of judging at Dublin: a wonderful privilege.

My father and stepmother were at the show as usual that first year I judged. I took with me Jennifer, to whom I was then engaged, as I knew what a wonderful experience Dublin would be for her. We all stayed at The Hermitage, which was where all the judges were accommodated in those days. It was an old-fashioned, but high-class hotel with a wonderful reputation for cuisine. On that first night, however, I was far too excited – and nervous – to eat much. The Judge had told me at the White City that in 1955 for the first time he was going to invite the senior judge simply to concentrate on conformation while the junior, younger judge, would do the riding in each class. My senior judge was a very experienced farmer and dealer from Shropshire, Ted Davies, the father of the Ted Davies who is a distinguished judge today. Whether the old boy, from whom I learnt a great deal, did not understand Judge Wylie's intentions or whether he was just obstinate I do not know, but he decided to ride every horse himself. Other senior judges followed suit so, sadly, the judge's plan never really came about, but it is good to see it increasingly introduced in Britain now. There is no doubt that this is the way for a young judge to learn.

The great day for the showing enthusiasts was, of course, the Thursday when the Weight and Overall Championships were judged in the main arena, the jumping enclosure. Despite the fact that the judging commenced at 10.30 a.m. the stand on the Committee Box side would be packed, the crowd showing as much interest and enthusiasm as at an average show the crowd shows for the main jumping event. The atmosphere is electric, everyone voicing his or her opinion and, inevitably, airing their criticism of the judging – or the riding of the judges. To gallop round that great arena, a full half-mile round, is an unforgettable experience; but often, too, one can feel that one has made a mistake. In the small outside rings a horse can look very attractive. It is obviously sound, has quality, but in those small rings outside it is not easy to see whether it can really gallop. With luck in the big ring it shows that it *can* gallop, but it is also possible that it cannot; in which case one looks very foolish if it is completely out-galloped by a horse which it has beaten in the small ring. I once went so far as to suggest to Judge Wylie that the judges need not finally place the top two horses until they have seen them gallop in the main arena, but nothing came of the suggestion, though I had the impression that he agreed, especially when he saw one of his own horses, originally placed second, show up the winner in the big arena. As can be imagined it is a great occasion when one finds that one is the senior weight judge and responsible for the final judging.

I was fortunate in that on the third occasion I was invited to judge – middleweights – my co-judge was Colonel Tony Murray-Smith, at that time Master of the Quorn, who was paying his first visit to Dublin, which meant that I was the senior. Although, obviously, I enjoyed the experience enormously, it was not an entirely happy occasion. The senior judge in the heavyweight section was a well known dealer. It seemed to me that he was determined to put up a big raw-boned chestnut belonging to another well known dealer. It was certainly a good hunter-type but not, in my opinion, a show horse. It lacked quality and, as I saw it, turned out one of its front feet. My anxiety was that if it was put up in the heavyweight section it would almost inevitably win the overall Championship – at that time there was a tendency to choose the heavyweight – as the dealer judge's influence would be stronger than ever, and one of my co-judges for the Championship was obviously on very familiar terms with him, and likely to support him. A good sort of hunter, I had to admit, but I just could not see him winning in the show ring in England, in the likely event of his being sold to an English stable. I could, however, just hear the pundits back in England asking who on earth had put that horse up in Dublin!

In the overall Championship each judge rides all the horses that he has not previously ridden so that they can be properly compared. The big chestnut, only a five-year-old, was obviously beginning to tire which frequently happens with young horses after they have galloped two or three times round that great arena, especially, as is frequently the case at

Dublin, if the going is heavy. (How furious Judge Wylie used to be if his precious jumping enclosure was badly cut up!) From the beginning I had found this big horse's mouth a little wooden, not unusual with a young horse at Dublin. Having taken him at a steady full canter down the far side, as we turned into the straight in front of the Committee Box I switched him into top gear. Halfway up the straight, just as I was approaching the Committee Box, flat out, unbelievably two members of the arena party walked straight across the narrow gap between the rails and one of the Irish banks, carrying a show-jumping pole. I had to make a very quick decision: I could try to pull up – obviously impossible at the pace I was going; swerve right round the bank – which almost certainly meant knocking over the stewards standing in the centre; or attempt to get through the gap between the pole and the rails – not more than ten feet. I attempted to steer to the left, but suddenly the horse's mouth seemed to go numb: I could not turn him. There was nothing for it: I would have to jump the pole, carried at shoulder height. But at the last moment the horse swerved sharp left, made the gap and, producing a braking system quite unexpectedly effective, stopped dead facing the delightful box hedge that surrounds the arena, hurling me head first into the pink and yellow Antirrhinums. Obviously there was no way this horse could now be champion. But when I apologised to the dealer judge he insisted, to my surprise, that I had no need to worry as, 'I am sure your middleweight' – the horse that Tony Murray-Smith and I had put up in the middleweight section – 'is our champion': so we were all agreed! The big chestnut did come to England, but never appeared in the show ring, though it later did quite well eventing. More than once my leg was pulled by the more perceptive for putting paid successfully, if somewhat dramatically, to any chance that the chestnut might have had!

My last two invitations to Dublin were to act as referee. For a senior judge this is the ideal job. One struts around, immaculate in one's riding kit, looking very important, enjoying all the Irish hospitality, yet the chances are that one will never have to ride a horse or reach a decision. On my very last appearance at Dublin two judges in one of the weight classes quite deliberately decided to disagree to ensure that the referee was called in! Needless to say, I was in the bar at that moment but the call reached me and I hurried into the ring. Having watched the class from the ringside I had no doubt which horse should win; but the judges insisted that I should ride them both, which I did, in a rainstorm, without any untoward incident. That was the last time that I had the privilege to judge at Dublin, just twenty-five years since I had first so nervously judged the middleweights with Ted Davies. But what an experience it had been! Although, sadly, the standard of the horses is not as good as it was – all the best young Irish-bred horses seem to have been sold out of Ireland before they have even had a saddle on their backs – the atmosphere is still unique, greater than at any other horse show in the world. It is just an unforgettable experience for any visitor; but even more so for anyone fortunate enough to be invited to judge.

Belfast

I was privileged, too, to judge at Balmoral, the beautiful showground at Belfast. My first experience was inauspicious. My very first class was the four-year-old class judged in the second ring, which was on a slight slope. My co-judge, a great show rider, the late Harry Bonner, and I agreed that there was really only one horse in the class. We duly brought it in first. Harry Bonner insisted that I start riding from the top, while he started at the bottom of the line. As I approached this nice young chestnut four-year-old its rider hissed at me, 'I should throw that away', indicating my stick. I handed it to my steward. I went up to the horse, was about to put my foot in the stirrup when the rider advised rather more firmly. 'I shouldn't get on that way. I'll give you a leg.' As I landed in the saddle the horse took a step backwards down the slope and went over backwards, landing right on top of me; not content with that giving me a kick on the thigh as it got up. As the groom caught the horse its rider helped me up. 'Didn't like the colour of your breeches', he said – a brand new pair, canary yellow! 'No objection to my hat?' I commented cynically, rubbing my thigh. The rider seemed astonished that I did not want to remount his horse. To pacify the rider, Harry Bonner, sportingly and gallantly, rode his horse, and with his masterly skill, proved that it was the best horse in the class.

Many years later there was an amusing sequence to this incident. I was walking down one of the arcades at Ballsbridge when I was approached by an Irishman who asked me if he was correct in thinking that I was Dorian Williams. Did I remember some years ago judging at the show in Belfast? I assured him that I did.

'Do you recall being thrown in the ring?'

'I remember very well a horse coming over backwards with me', I told him.

'Well', he said, 'there was a neighbour of mine present that day and she insisted that if I saw you at Dublin I was to speak to you. You see, my unfortunate neighbour was pregnant at the time.'

'Yes?' I really could not see what this had to do with me.

'Well, it was like this, sir: she was that shocked when she saw you thrown and the horse rolling on top of you that she gave birth there and then.'

'Good heavens!' I said, suitably astonished, 'in the show ground?'

'Behind the stands, sir; and what is more, it was twins!'

I hardly knew what to say, and certainly had difficulty not to laugh. 'I hope everything was all right, that – that they're doing well. It must have been fifteen years ago.'

'It was, sir, and I'm glad to say they're both fine; two splendid boys. And their mother said as I was to tell you, sir, that in view of the circumstances in which they were born she decided to call one Dorian and the other William, and she said she was sure that you would not mind.'

No, indeed! And I wish them the very best. But surely it could happen only in Ireland.

Chapter 10

Paradise Amongst the Problems

South Africa: Johannesburg
In 1958, two years after I had first judged at Dublin I received an invitation to judge at the Rand Easter Show at Johannesburg. I was offered a first-class flight together with accommodation at a first-class hotel for the fortnight's duration of the show. I was informed, however, that if I liked to exchange my first-class ticket for two tourist-class tickets I could then bring my wife, who would also be accommodated free. Jennifer agreed to come with alacrity – the last time that she was ever to agree with alacrity to fly anywhere. It was a long flight, made longer by our having to change from the old BOAC to Sabena at Brussels. The whole journey took just under thirty hours.

We were met by the show secretary, an extremely impressive man of the name of Laubscher – a rugby international – and his young assistant. Also there to greet us was Tony Wilson, the younger brother of Peter Wilson who was Chairman of the Stock Exchange and Master of the Rand Hunt. Tony, unmarried, was one of Harry Oppenheimer's right-hand men, later to become a close friend of ours. Hospitably, knowing how tired we must be, they insisted that we should retire to our suite in the hotel, order our dinner to be sent up when we wanted it, and go to bed early as they would be collecting us soon after 8.00 a.m. next morning to take us to the show ground. In fact, we fell asleep straight away not waking up until long past dinner time.

The show ground was most impressive, being part of a large exhibition centre covering at least twenty acres. The arena itself was spacious, big enough to hold two rings. The main stand, on the shady side, was exclusively for Members who had access to adequate rather than luxurious amenities. An open stand the other side was for the coloured, and free. Shortly before the start of the first class that I was to judge the Chairman of the horse section appeared, profuse in his apologies for not being there to greet us earlier but he had 'had a little trouble at the mine and had to knock out the manager'. Colonel Faunce Tainton was someone straight out of Sapper or Buchan, in the Guards in the First World War but resident in South Africa ever since. Wearing a faded dark blue blazer and a battered trilby, he was big with a crumpled face and a little clipped moustache. We grew to like him immensely. He was kindness itself, had an old-fashioned, courteous charm, and in company was quiet and diffident. He took a great fancy to Jennifer and nothing was ever too much trouble in helping us. He insisted on the show hiring a car for us, thus making us completely independent; and from the way we were treated at the hotel it was obvious that he had had a word with the management.

The show being run principally for the white population, apart from the free seats 'the other side', it was only when I went to a post office to apply for a local driving licence that I first became aware of apartheid. We were shocked at the way the whites pushed the blacks off the pavements; and I was even more shocked when taking my place in the queue at the post office behind an elderly black a police officer came along and seizing the black by the arm threw him to the back of the queue. Instinctively, I was about to protest but, suddenly aware of where I was, thought better of it.

We enjoyed the show enormously, making many friends, some of whom have remained friends to this day. The classes for the most part were very large and when it was hot, which it mostly was, very tiring to judge; but the show never ran late, invariably finishing in time for us to be whisked off to the Inanda Club, the focal point for the equestrian set in Johannesburg, or to one of the beautiful private houses situated in the prosperous suburbs. I was kept so busy that we never managed to get to Kruger Park, but I had a day's hunting with the Rand Hunt – a drag – and must have jumped forty fences. Jennifer was disappointed at our hosts refusing to let her hunt because of the occasional lethal potholes. Luckily I never encountered one. We also went to the Hunt Ball, at which I had to make a speech, as I did at the official show lunch, which was attended by the President, Dr Vervoltd. As we came from England he seemed most interested to meet us, speaking to us for all of ten minutes, trying to explain his plans for separate development. However repugnant they might appear to most people they certainly sounded from his lips considerably less horrific than portrayed in the western press: almost idealistic, in fact.

For the first time ever an Afrikaaner, a farmer, had been persuaded to enter a horse in one of the classes, which resulted in my one embarrassing moment. It was little more than a pony, which was why it found itself in my second row when I lined up the class. Immediately my steward informed me that it would be politic to move it up to the front row, which I did; but this meant that I had to ride it. Apart from the fact that my legs almost touched the ground either side of this butty little pony it soon became apparent that the aids that I applied were entirely alien to the Africaaner's. Whatever I did it just went faster and faster, apparently having no intention of stopping. As I passed the line I called to the owner, asking how I should stop: but by the time that he had given me his advice I was 100 yards away. Eventually, in desperation, I just rode the horse into the back of the front line and came to a crash halt. Fortunately none of the horses that I had banged into kicked; but it was with great relief that I dismounted, apologising for my inadequate riding.

Finally it was time to return to England. We had been given a delightful farewell party at Harry Oppenheimer's house the night before we left and there had been a round of visits before reaching the airport. We were quite exhausted, but as we boarded our plane we had little idea of the ordeal that lay ahead.

The first unpleasant experience was landing at Leopoldville, our first stop. As we started our descent we ran into an electric storm, and our aircraft was actually struck by lightning. The violent lurch and a sudden drop of several hundred feet were not pleasant, but what was more worrying was the fact that the airport itself had been struck by lightning, plunging it into complete darkness and, presumably, cutting off all its electricity, which obviously made landing difficult, and the conditions when we had landed – safely, to our relief – very unpleasant. After an hour or so on the ground groping around for a cup of coffee we were guided back to our plane by torches to set off on the long haul to Geneva.

Ten hours later, we began our descent into Geneva and as the weather was perfect we could see the whole of the French Mediterranean coastline with the snow-covered Alps in the background. Approaching Geneva Airport, however, we encountered dense fog despite which, a little to my surprise, we were obviously attempting a landing. Slowly, laboriously, the engines throbbing, we dropped through the fog which seemed wholly to envelop us, giving one a feeling of claustrophobia – imprisonment almost. Jennifer sat with her eyes shut, her hands clenched, while I peered out of my porthole. For some moments I thought that I was looking at streaks of rain running vertically down the window pane, but suddenly I realised that we were flying amongst the trees! They were saplings, right by the side of the plane. That we must in a few seconds hit one was inevitable, yet surprisingly I had no sense of fear at that moment, only frustration, annoyance even; such was the feeling of inevitability that one's senses seemed numbed. The next moment there was a terrifying crash as one of the plane's wings hit a tree. The plane heeled over until it was completely on its side; at the same time all the crockery and glass in the lockers were hurtled to the floor. The engines roared deafeningly, the plane shuddered, then miraculously righted itself, soaring upwards through the fog and out into the blue sky. As the passengers sat there, tense and shaken, we flew round in two big circles before, incredibly, attempting a second landing, which, miraculously, was achieved perfectly.

Nobody seemed to want to speak, as we disembarked, but everyone was perspiring freely; one or two women were weeping. It was eight o'clock in the morning. We were all ushered into the restaurant where we were immediately offered bacon and eggs which, not surprisingly, nobody seemed inclined to accept. After a short time the crew joined us, sitting down at the table next to ours. The pilot, who only looked about twenty-two, suddenly slumped over the table, having, presumably, fainted, but with the ministrations of his crew he was quickly revived, drank a cup of coffee and, with the rest of the crew, left the restaurant.

We were astonished and, if the truth were told, more than a little anxious, to find that he was to fly us on to Brussels. Again the weather for the flight was perfect – we could even see the Eiffel Tower as we flew over Paris – but again the weather deteriorated as we approached Brussels. This time as we commenced our descent we flew into a snowstorm. At the first attempt we overshot the runway, revving up violently just before the plane's wheels touched the tarmac. No one could doubt that the young pilot had managed brilliantly both at Geneva and Brussels, particularly at the former when somehow he managed to get his plane airbound again having obviously been off beam as we came down through the mountains, but for the passengers the experience had, to say the least, been extremely alarming. The very thought of yet another flight, from Brussels to London, albeit in another plane, horrified Jennifer; indeed, I think that she would have preferred to swim the channel rather than fly, had it not been for the thought of our one-year-old-son, Piers, whom she had not seen for nearly a month, waiting at home. Ever since that occasion Jennifer has avoided flying if she possibly can.

We were invited to Johannesburg again two or three years later. This time Jennifer was invited to judge as well which meant that we were offered two first-class tickets. Despite this Jennifer was still very apprehensive. I consulted our doctor who gave her pills of various colours which she was to take at regular intervals throughout the twenty-six-hour flight. She would hardly know, he assured her, that she had been in the air. But this was not the case at all. Though relaxed she was wide awake all the time, thoroughly enjoying the wonderful menus provided for first-class passengers; the dinner between Frankfurt and Nairobi, of smoked salmon and duckling with fruit meringue for sweet, washed down by champagne, claret and liqueurs; the 'light meal', between Nairobi and Johannesburg of fresh pineapple, grilled fillet steak or seafood pancake Nazlina, assorted cheeses, again accompanied by champagne. On landing at Johannesburg, however, she fell asleep for three days! Fortunately she was not involved at the beginning of our visit, which on this occasion lasted nearly seven weeks – too long in our opinion, despite everyone's kindness and hospitality.

My first assignment was to commentate at the show jumping National Championships on the outskirts of Johannesburg. On this occasion we were accommodated at the home of Tony Wilson, who had succeeded Faunce Tainton as Chairman of the Rand Show Horse section. He lived in a most beautiful house at Inanda with a delightful garden and swimming-pool. It was probably the nearest to paradise that we have ever been. The house was presided over by a faithful valet-cum-butler-cum-chauffeur, James, who was also Tony's best friend. He was black as ebony, small, gentle, with wonderful wit and prepared to do anything for 'massa' or his friends. When Tony came to England each year for the Royal Show, James came too. They always used to stay with us which delighted the girls who worked for us, as when they came down to the stables at 6.30 a.m. they would find that James had already done all the work. There was also a gardener-cum-chef, Joe, and a splendid coloured woman who had been engaged especially to look after Jennifer. It was with real sadness that we left Tony's at the end of the show, but we were anxious to visit Kruger Park before flying on to Port Elizabeth.

We had been invited to stay with a great character, Ida Illingworth who, as a mistress at Roedean, had set off thirty years earlier with her friend, Nell, to drive from England to Capetown – the first ladies, not surprisingly, to achieve this incredible journey. Falling in love with South Africa, they decided to stay – doubtless to the loss of Roedean – and settled down at a little estate at White River, on the edge of the Park, to breed Welsh ponies, having imported a lovely little stallion, Valiant, from England. A near neighbour, Mrs Stevenson-Hamilton, acted as our guide in the Park in which we spent three and a half days. We could not possibly have had a better guide; Mrs Stevenson-Hamilton had gone out to South Africa as a schoolgirl to visit a friend and had met, fallen in love with and married the first Warden of the Park. Virtually the founder of the first game park in Africa, he was nearly forty years older than his wife, but it was an extremely happy marriage, though, of course, he died when his wife was quite a young woman. Not only was she extremely talented – a sculptress, a poetess, a writer – but like her husband she was a dedicated naturalist. Our visit to the Park was an unforgettable experience providing us with the opportunity of seeing just about everything there was to see; but for me, exciting as were the lions, hyena, cheetah, rhino, giraffe and wild dog – oddly enough the rarest of all – it was the exquisite little pied king-fisher, that we watched on a branch barely five yards from our van, that fascinated me most.

We only had tourist tickets for the flight to Port Elizabeth, where we had also been invited to judge, so to keep within the weight we had to carry as much as we possibly could, eventually looking like walking Christmas trees. This did not matter too much at Johannesburg but at Port Elizabeth where it seems always to be blowing a gale it was all that we could do to make our way across the tarmac from the plane to the airport buildings.

Johannesburg is not exactly sophisticated, and Port Elizabeth is considerably less so. The show had not the status of the Rand Show, nor was it so professionally organised; for instance, Jennifer had to judge a hack class in a small ring which not only had a six-inch hose pipe lying right across the ring – goodness knows why – but had, at the edge of the ring, a helicopter giving flights to the public. Jennifer swore that she would never again complain about the distractions during a hack class back home, such as moving show-jumping poles and riders walking the course. The most amusing incident, however, was on the day the State's President visited the show. It was a brief visit but when he was ready to depart his car was not ready. The chauffeur was called over the loudspeaker, not once, not twice, but thrice. Eventually in a cloud of dust the black limousine, with its motor-cycle escort, swept into the arena – only to run out of petrol on the far side!

As always we made very good friends who were kind and helpful, particularly Peter Ogden and his wife who arranged for us to be loaned a car in order that we could drive down to Plattenburg Bay where we stayed for a few days; we were accommodated in a somewhat primitive hotel, but, despite moderate weather, enjoyed some exciting surfing and a visit to another wild life park. We should have liked to continue to Cape Town, but had to return to Blomfontain where Jennifer was judging Welsh ponies. There was time for just forty-eight hours back at Inanda with Tony Wilson before setting off for home.

During those forty-eight hours two remarks were made to me in very different circumstances, giving me food for thought on the way home. I was sitting in the car with James on the morning of our departure, waiting for Jennifer outside the hairdresser's, when suddenly, apropos of nothing, James said 'Massa must understand: here we happy – in Tanzania they not happy.' I had carefully avoided any political conversation. I said nothing now. I knew that James went with Tony Wilson when he was accompanying Harry Oppenheimer to Tanzania; just as I knew that every eighteen months or so – almost without warning – he returned to his own tribe in the north for four or five months.

The previous day we had been to the township of Soweto. We were shown all round by the manager – who was not a supporter of the government – and been both depressed by much obvious squalor, poverty and degradation, yet also impressed by the comparative wealth in some areas – big cars, servants, often due to the fact that no whites are allowed to farm near the township, the franchise for the farm products going only to coloured farmers. Back in his office, the manager expressed the hope that we would report approvingly back home in Britain. When rather vaguely I said that I would do my best he told me in quiet resigned tones: 'You see we had a young journalist from one of your famous national dailies last week: he was here for two days and seemed impressed, but when I said that I hoped that he would report favourably, he told me that he could not as he had been sent out to report *un*favourably!'

I left South Africa on that occasion depressed and confused.

Pietermaritzburg

Our last visit was in 1975 when we were invited to judge at the Royal Show, Pietermaritzburg, in Natal. Generously flown out first-class we found our flight was particularly interesting – apart from the smoked salmon, scampi in creamed brandy sauce and cutlet of veal with smoked ham, mushrooms and cheese; yes, those menus have been carefully preserved – because of our landing at Nairobi. About five minutes before we were due to land the captain announced over the intercom that he now had no further responsibility for the landing. He had handed over to ground control for an entirely automatic landing. We were both agreed that it was the smoothest landing that we had ever experienced. We had to spend one night in Johannesburg before flying on to Pietermaritzburg so were able to pay a final visit to Tony Wilson at Inanda. Sadly he died a year or two later, though we were to see him once again when, with the devoted James, he stayed with us for the Royal Show in England.

Our hosts at Pietermaritzburg were Hubert von Klemperer, Chairman of the Show's Horse Section, and his wife, Meg. Their charming house, colonial style with an attractive terraced garden, was only four or five miles from the show ground, but must have been 1,000 feet up, approached by a winding road through a forest. Not its least interesting feature was the narrow gauge railway that climbed to the quarry above us. At night we heard it chugging and hooting its way up the hill and it seemed as if it were coming right through our bedroom. The house was quite isolated with beautiful tracks through the woodlands where Hubert took us riding.

The Royal Show, despite its title, is more like a smaller county show in England. It has a happy relaxed atmosphere and is run in far from formal surroundings. The show lasted eight days, everyone of which we enjoyed; the classes were interesting and varied and there was enough free time to explore the neighbourhood, including a visit to another national park. Driving up one track a huge lion leapt down from a bank right in front of our car. I only just missed it as it leaped back up the bank.

The standard of the exhibits in the show classes was not very high, but we were impressed by the enormous enthusiasm. The standard in the jumping, however, on which I had been asked to commentate, was much higher and we were delighted when Tony Wilson's really good horse called Xenophon, ridden by his young world-class rider, Mickey Louw, won the Grand Prix after an exciting jump-off, beat-

ing Gonda Beatrix (Butters) and Anneli Wucherpfennig
(Drummond-Hay, both well known in Britain.

To help in the judging of some of my classes I had the
services of a very able Dawn Mackenzie, the wife of a big
farmer in the Karkloof mountains. They kindly invited us to
spend a day at their farm which bordered on a large lake where
Maurice Mackenzie kept an outboard motor boat. It was
suggested that we might go across the lake as it had been
rumoured that on the other side a white rhinoceros had just
had a calf which no one had yet seen. We were lucky. For
several minutes we watched the mother pushing the calf along
in front of her, at quite a pace even though the calf was only
two or three days old. Apparently the calf never follows its
mother, but for reasons of safety and precaution is pushed in
front, which presumably explains that great horn! When we
boarded our boat Maurice Mackenzie was helped by his farm
manager, a splendid looking Zulu all of six feet tall. While we
were watching them prepare the boat the manager and his boss
were chatting. As we set off across the lake Maurice Mackenzie asked us if we would like to know what they had been
talking about, in the Zulus' native language. He explained that
Zulus had this remarkable ability to sum up a stranger's
character and personality on sight, giving him or her an
appropriate name. He had, apparently, immediately
christened us. I was NODUMEHLEZI: 'He whose mind thunders
even while he relaxes', a description that I could not possibly
deny. Jennifer's was more subtle – HLEKA BAFASI: 'The laughter
of woman: a bird which smiles even when a smile is not
intended'. Being shy Jennifer often gives people the
impression that she is not appreciating the seriousness of what
is said, rather looking relaxed and unconcerned. We were told
that the Zulus considered their own culture very superior to
the 'whites' and had no wish whatever to be absorbed into the
white culture and civilisation. Confusing again – and
thought-provoking.

Mary Oppenheimer, then Mrs Bill Johnson, was a competitor whom we had met on previous visits to South Africa.
Very kindly she invited us to their seaside home on the
outskirts of Durban for the weekend before we flew home.
Meg von Klemperer drove us down, arriving at this

sumptuous villa in time for lunch. As Harry was not arriving until the next day the five of us, Mrs Oppenheimer, Mary, Meg and ourselves sat down to lunch by ourselves, on the patio; each of us had a coloured servant behind our chair, and the service of the whole meal was supervised by a European major domo, dressed in a smart white suit. At the end of the meal we rose to depart to the drawing-room for coffee, but the major domo signalled to me that I was expected to remain, on my own, for a liqueur and a cigar. As he cut my cigar the major domo said that he hoped that I would not be offended if he asked me to sign his 'book' – a visitor's book or even an autograph book, I assumed. To my surprise he produced a well-worn copy of *Pendley and a Pack of Hounds* which I had had published in 1959. Apparently he had relations living at Mentmore only five miles from Pendley, where we then lived. They had sent him a copy some fifteen years earlier; he had kept it ever since, but never expected to 'meet the author and invite him to sign it in person in South Africa'. Nor I!

It has to be admitted that in the ten years or so between our last two visits we had noticed very considerable progress in the apartheid development. Every other car seemed to be driven by a coloured or black; very few shops or hotels appeared to ban coloureds or blacks. Our impression was that it was very much a case of *festina lente*: at least there was progress.

Twice, regrettably, I had to refuse invitations to judge in Zimbabwe, then Rhodesia, on the way home from South Africa as I was unable to be away from home so long. For the same reason I could not fit in a visit to Kenya. I did, however, spend an enjoyable holiday in Morocco, and a less enjoyable one in Algiers which I found very dreary and was left in little doubt that British visitors were not exactly popular. In Morocco I blatantly used my position as Chairman of the British Horse Society to gain access to the Royal Stables in Rabat, an immensely enjoyable experience which not only gave us the opportunity to see all the exquisitely beautiful horses in their stables – and twenty-seven of the stallions specially paraded before me as I stood on a decorated dais – but also the saddle room with its unique jewelled saddlery and the riding hall with its mosaic walls. No less thrilling was the fantasia, in the presence of the King, at Marakesh; more

amusing were our efforts to arrange to go for a ride along the
dunes in front of the Hotel Hacienda at Agadir, when we were
only allowed actually to ride after we had been given a test by a
sixteen-year-old Arab youth. Rather unsportingly the Chairman of the British Horse Society declined! Had I failed that test
could our friends ever have resisted spreading the news
through the horse world back home in England?

The continent of Africa is one of contrasts and contradic-
tions. It is such a pity that some of the paranoia and bias cannot
be replaced with a little understanding and realism. That
remarkable continent is, surely, paradise on earth; but so
much of it, too, is conflict and controversy. One very small
gleam of light can be seen in the increasing number of
coloureds and blacks now riding in top-class equestrian
events. The backwardness of the African tribes has sometimes
been attributed to the fact that they never used a wheel or rode
a horse. Could this be the beginning of the beginning?

Chapter 11

Down Under – and Back

Australia

At the White City in 1966 we were introduced to Alec Creswick, now Sir Alexander Creswick, the President of the Australian Equestrian Federation. He invited Jennifer and myself round to the apartment that he had taken in Belgravia to drinks with him and his wife, who bred ponies. To our delight he told us that we had been asked round so that he could invite us to judge at the Royal Melbourne Show the following year. Naturally, we were happy to accept, regarding it as a great honour, as nobody from Britain had previously been invited to judge. It seemed an ideal opportunity to take a holiday on the way in some exotic place that we would not normally ever be able to visit. We decided, therefore, to travel via Honolulu.

We were not greatly impressed with the famous Waikiki beach. Apart from the endless glutinous drone of Hawaiian music wafting out at us from loudspeakers wherever we went, we were accommodated on the twenty-seventh floor of a very modern hotel, which was not at all to Jennifer's liking. She was convinced that she could feel the hotel swaying whenever the wind blew, which it did all the time. After two or three days I enquired at the hotel information desk whether there were not a quieter hotel out of town. We were given the name of a 'small and select' hotel the other side of the island, so we hired a car and drove across. It appeared charming, though really not much more than an up-market motel, built round a simple square with a pool in the middle, flanked by exotic flowering shrubs. We unpacked, washed and changed and we went downstairs to explore. There not being very much to explore we sought out the bar for a drink before dinner.

'Bar?' exclaimed an astonished concièrge. 'Bar! There's no bar here – this is a Mormon hotel.' In fact, we could not even get a cup of tea or coffee, as those were considered stimulants; which in the end was to save us a good deal of money as we bought our gin and whisky – and coffee – at a local drug store, and served our own drinks on the balcony of our room. Despite the 'prohibition' we very much enjoyed ourselves at this little Mormon Hotel which we had more or less to ourselves, including a wonderful beach. I shall never forget the exotic fruit dishes and fruit drinks served in the attractive Hawaiian-style restaurant, by the most beautiful Samoan girls, so lithe, so pretty, so anxious to please, always with a shy smile. They were, I think, the loveliest people I have ever met. We had an amusing morning, too, when, having inspected the splendid white Mormon Church, we were invited to see a film on the history of the Mormons. The two of us sat alone in the back row of a huge cinema and after a time we became rather childishly giggly, not knowing how we could escape, without appearing rude. Needless to say we were not converted, but were pleased to learn something of the Mormons and their remarkable history and to be convinced that the widely broadcast story that Mormons have numerous wives is entirely without foundation.

Melbourne
On returning to Honolulu we found that we had made a mistake over the date and time of our flight to Tonga and Sydney. It is easy enough to make a mistake as, *en route*, one first gains a day then loses one – or is it the other way round? At any rate we had to stay another night in our skyscraper hotel, but this time on the thirty-eighth floor, even more to Jennifer's alarm. The view, of course, was fabulous, but Jennifer found little compensation in the fact that we could actually see Pearl Harbor! Thanks to the mix-up with our flights we arrived in Sydney a day later than anticipated. Instead of a direct flight by jet to Melbourne we had to fly in an ancient Viscount with two stops on the way – a far worse flight in Jennifer's opinion than the two mammoth hops from Britain. She was somewhat compensated by the huge bouquet of flowers 'from a fellow pony breeder' that greeted us in our suite. Obviously Mrs

Creswick, we thought; yet to our surprise when we entered the dining-room and were shown to our table at one end of the room the Creswicks, at the other end of the room, ignored us. At the show on the first morning we were walking down one of the avenues when, as we crossed another avenue we heard a voice shout 'Jennifer! Hallo! Welcome to Victoria!' It was a school-friend whom Jennifer had not met since she had left school. She was leading a thoroughbred stallion with which she explained, she had just won second prize. They were happily chatting away when to our astonishment an official came up, tapped Jennifer on the shoulder and said, 'I'm afraid judges must not be seen talking to exhibitors.' Innocently Jennifer started to explain that she was judging ponies not thoroughbred stallions, but the official summarily pointed Jennifer's friend in the direction of the stables. Despite a number of not dissimilar experiences, despite the bad weather – on two days the show was abandoned – despite, too, my having to judge a class of hacks (hunters, as we would term them in Britain) while a lady clad in a tight white leather costume was being fired across the arena from a gun and despite the length of our day on the showground – it started at 8.00 a.m. and finished at 10.00 p.m. which meant that, apart from the two wet days, we had no time off – despite all these things we thoroughly enjoyed the show, chiefly because people were very kind to us, but not a little because we formed a great affection for the Chairman, David Knox, who was the image, in appearance and behaviour, of David Niven.

We both had enormous classes, seldom less than sixty. One excellent idea was arranging for all the hacks (hunters) to parade in the arena the evening before the show for the judge to decide whether they should be judged as heavyweights or lightweights. In Britain they would be lightweights and middleweights, as heavyweights as known in Britain do not exist in Australia. The difficulty for the judge was that most horses appeared in about six different classes – ridden by an amateur, owner-ridden, horse-ridden in equipment owned by rider, best turned-out – which made it difficult to remember exactly in which order the horses had been placed previously. For the first and only time I had to jot down on a piece of paper the numbers of my placed horses, so that I would not get it wrong in a subsequent class – always assuming that the horse's appearance and performance was the same as in a previous class. Jennifer's great problem was having to judge a sixty-strong class on the fifteen-feet-wide running track because the arena had become waterlogged. Halfway through the show she completed her judging of the pony classes, finally giving the championship to a pony that, as it turned out, belonged to Mrs Creswick. When we went into dinner that night we were immediately greeted by the Creswicks, inviting us to join them at their table. They explained that they dare not be seen talking to us until the judging had finished. Apparently there had previously been so much graft amongst the judges who were all from New South Wales or South Australia that it had been decided to import judges from as far away as possible as they would know none of the exhibits. This, of course, explained everything. We had had an introduction to a wealthy man called Cox who had a stud about sixty miles from Melbourne. We were particularly keen to visit his stud as we had heard that he had unusually interesting ideas on feeding and nutrition and that his stallions had an exception-ally high fertility rate – over 90 per cent compared with less than 65 per cent in Britain; all his stallions, which included the Queen's Phaeton, running out with the mares. The organisa-tion did not seem too keen on us visiting Mr Cox as he appeared to be somewhat *persona non grata* with the set that ran the show. It appeared to us that the claim so often made that there is no class distinction, no snobbery in Australia, does not really hold up, especially in certain states. Eventually we played truant one day, and well worthwhile it was; except that on our return we found that we had missed the spectacle of the Chairman knocking out the Show Director at the end of the show in the Committee Room as he had shut his office too early, locking the Chairman's coat inside!

At a reception held at the end of the show Jennifer was surprised and delighted to be presented with a silver brooch as a token of appreciation from the exhibitors – who, presum-ably, were relieved to have judging of complete integrity. The Committee obviously felt that they ought to do something, too, so someone was surreptitiously despatched to fetch a couple of the magnificent sashes placed round the necks of all the champions. They were duly produced, one for each of us; but when the Chairman hung Jennifer's round her neck the wording on the sash, for all to see, proclaimed 'Champion In-calf Heifer'.

My own final experience was a little less fortunate. The great Championship on the final day is the Garry Owen Trophy – of sufficient importance to be headlined in all the major daily papers – which is judged solely on turn-out. Having completed my difficult task I had just placed the sash round the winner when the lady standing about fourth, who had just been presented with her rosette by a steward, shouted out, 'You're a disgrace. You're not fit to judge anywhere. Goodness knows why they brought you all the way from England. The sooner you go back there the better. You obviously don't know that I've won the Garry Owen for the last two years.' Whereupon she threw her rosette at me.

'Perhaps you have madam', I could not resist calling back, 'but this year I happened to see you bucked off in the collecting ring, the evidence of which is still to be seen on the seat of your breeches'– which she had failed to conceal even at the sitting trot!–'and this is supposed to be a Turn-Out Championship.'

I considered it quite a joke but the Committee, quite unnecessarily, insisted on making a public apology at the final reception, which I found embarrassing. I would have been quite content if her father, the Show Director, had quite forcibly removed the dirt from the seat of her breeches.

We had decided to spend twenty-four hours in Sydney on the way home, in case we never had a further opportunity. Friends kindly met us at the airport and drove us round to see the sights. Unfortunately the rain was so torrential that we could see nothing, not even the famous bridge; but luckily we had the opportunity to see it under more favourable circumstances a few years later.

Singapore
Unfortunately we were unable to accept an invitation to judge at the great Royal Sydney Show in 1970, as that year it coincided with the Badminton Horse Trials. A year or two earlier I had received a rap on the knuckles from the BBC for preferring to attend my own point-to-point rather than cover

the show-jumping phase at Badminton. In those days the event finished on the Saturday. The BBC had been unimpressed by my suggestion that unless I maintained my own equestrian activities I would be unable to talk with authority on equestrian activities televised by the BBC. My father and stepmother had judged at Sydney and had rated it as one of their most unforgettable experiences. I was delighted, therefore, to be asked to Sydney in 1979 to commentate at the new Benson and Hedges Show Jumping which was being held as part of the Festival of Sydney. I went on my own and, British Airways being joint sponsors, I travelled first-class – Langouste Thermidor, Brocketts *de dinde à la diable!* – stopping off for twenty-four hours at Singapore where I was accommodated by the Michael Tibbatts at their attractive house by the racecourse – Captain Tibbatts was secretary to the Bukit Timia Racecourse. They kindly gave a drinks party for the horsey community, which I greatly enjoyed, as I did breakfast next morning in the garden, shared with a pair of beautiful golden oriels flirting in the trees above me. They also showed me some of the often fascinating sights of Singapore.

Sydney
The new show-jumping event at Sydney was an attempt by Ted Dwyer, President of New South Wales Show Jumping Association, and Henry Rundle, the Australian FEI representative, to put show jumping on the map as a popular sport. It was considered highly successful. I enjoyed it all immensely despite the fact that the conditions for my efforts were so different from those I was used to at home. The chief commentator, John Nash, was a charming and extremely good-looking sometime actor who had his own radio programme. As in America, the commentator is expected to give a running commentary throughout a round, actually while a competitor is jumping, which I did not easily take to. Nor did I find it easy to collect information about the riders and horses, other than such as John Fahey, Guy Creighton, Greg Eurell, Di Dawson and the Grand Prix winner Marianne Gilchrist, all of whom had visited Europe; and, of course, Caroline Bradley, Malcolm Pyrah and Derek Ricketts who had been invited out from Britain to compete on borrowed horses. I also did a

number of radio broadcasts, in which my way of speaking apparently attracted much comment, both favourable and unfavourable, from listeners. Off-duty highlights were a visit to Ross and Ann Fields on Pacific Road Palm Beach, an extensive tour of Sydney with John Nash and his American wife and a most exciting trip round the harbour in fairly lively weather.

To my surprise and delight I was invited again to the Sydney Festival Show in 1980, and on this occasion Jennifer also was invited to judge 'ponies'. On the way out, to break the journey, we stopped off at Singapore for two nights and three full days, which provided us with the unforeseen opportunity to accept an invitation to lunch at the Palace of the Sultan of Johore, across the causeway. It was arranged at short notice by a lady, whom we had met at a little reception organised for us, on the evening of our arrival. A few years earlier she had worked at the Palace as a kind of social secretary. The old Sultan, then rising eighty, was unable to walk as a result of a motor accident in which his wife had been killed eighteen months earlier; but he had now remarried, his new wife being his son's sister-in-law, a beautiful French-born lady, not yet thirty. We were to meet him at the smaller of his two palaces which overlooked his private zoo and his polo grounds. Shown into a large but rather dark room I was surprised to discover that the tiny little man seated on an upright chair at the corner of a massive table, but at least six feet away from it, wearing a loose linen dark blue suit and a cap similar to that worn by the Chinese, was none other than His Highness.

Greatly to my astonishment his first remark to me was 'I have read articles by you in *Horse and Hound*', after which he told me that he had hunted with the old Berkeley when he had been at Cambridge in the 1920s. As so much of that country is familiar to me we were soon in easy and animated conversation. He then told me that he was going to take us to see the new palace that he was building – each room of which was being lined with pink marble – before showing us his stables where he kept more than 200 horses and polo ponies: but first we were to see his zoo with the crocodiles and fifteen-inch high Chinese Water Deer. Finally we were to go to lunch with

him at his main Palace where we would see his collection of
cars – eighteen of them, all licensed – including the one in
which his wife was killed, in exactly the same condition as it
was after the accident, buckled, the windows splintered,
blood on the floor. Much to his new young wife's distress at
lunch he hardly ate anything himself, preferring to pass the
meal-time showing me, who had the privilege to sit next to
him, his 'treasures'. He would clap his hands and a lackey
immediately appeared, to be instructed to produce a special
book, an album of photographs, a jewelled sword, even a
copy of *Horse and Hound*, and finally two small Siamese
kittens.

'I see that you are advertising them for sale', remarked one
of his guests.

'That is true', said His Highness, 'but I have had no replies
to my advertisement.'

'Do you not think, Highness, that you are asking rather a lot
of money for two small kittens?'

'Five hundred dollars? Do you suggest that I ask too much? I
have to live, you know', and he gave me an impish wink.

Before we left I asked him when he was last in London. He
told me that he had not been back since 1923: 'And now it is
impossible for me to return: you see, the last time my
grandfather went he died, staying at the Dorchester Hotel; and
then when my father went for the Coronation he died, at
Grosvenor House; so obviously I dare not go back myself.' He
smiled impishly again, then added: 'But I would like to see the
hunting again.' Sadly this charming little man died himself the
following year, at his own Palace – not the new one, as it was
still unfinished. We were happy to have met him, and also,
briefly, his son who has recently been elected King of
Malaysia.

This time in Sydney I was invited to give television commentaries on the major event on each of the three days, to which
had been invited again riders from Britain, Ireland, and New
Zealand. The British riders this time were Ted and Liz Edgar
and Nick Skelton. The regular show-jumping commentator
was Rod Smith, whose two elder brothers were both international riders; he was extremely good, his homework being so

extensive that he had at least a foolscap page of information on each horse competing. This was splendid when he was doing the public address on the minor competitions; but it was not so satisfactory – from my point of view – when we were televising, as invariably he had not reached the end of his public address introduction by the time the horse on which I was supposed to be commentating was approaching the end of the course. I scarcely had time to do more than give out the faults! He did not, however, resent my asking him if he could at least get his introduction completed by the time the horse had reached the first fence, preferably before it had started. The first day's television was little more than a trailer, but on the second day we had a full house; on the third day the stadium gates had to be closed by midday. Indeed, I was even told that almost as many people failed to gain admission at Wentworth Park as were actually inside. I was reminded of the early days of show jumping on television in Britain when we experienced the startling rise in attendance.

Jennifer was a little embarrassed to find that the 'ponies' that she had been invited to judge were in fact harness classes. However, after agreeing with some diffidence to undertake the task she did, according to the opinions of the experts, an excellent job – though not unexpectedly had her leg properly pulled by Frank and Cynthia Haydon on her return.

The highlight of this visit for me, was an invitation to the Committee Box to watch a test match in the England–Australia series. Unbelievably I found myself at lunch sitting between the legendary Harold Larwood and Chairman of the English Selectors, Alec Bedser. I also met a very old friend from prep-school days, Derek Mendl. We had not met for over fifty years, but it might have been yesterday.

Again we were generously flown out and back first class – Strasbourg *foie gras* in pastry crust, breast of pheasant in truffled Madeira sauce – and had an excellent flight via Singapore, Bombay, Dubai and Paris, which Jennifer enjoyed as much as I did despite the fact that we flew direct, not breaking our journey anywhere. She did, however, feel that it was a very long way to go for a week so when kindly invited the following year we decided not to accept. It would in any case have been very difficult as I was suffering from an exceedingly painful frozen shoulder.

Return to Australia
I did, however, enjoy one further visit to Australia in 1982. Eric Ixer, who for many years was a senior course builder in England, now lived in Queensland where he was Warden of Andalucia Park on the Gold Coast about twenty miles from Brisbane, and Secretary of the Queensland Equestrian Federation. Having been asked to organise a show to coincide with the Commonwealth Games, which were being held in Brisbane, he kindly invited me to fly out to do the public address commentary, and possibly some broadcasts. I was happy to accept as no longer being Master of the Whaddon Chase Hunt it did not matter my missing a fortnight's cub-hunting in October. I decided to take the opportunity to pay a visit to Hong Kong *en route*, never having been there previously. I had friends there, and also a cousin who was a doctor.

Hong Kong
It is quite an experience landing in Hong Kong as one's plane literally swoops through the houses to the single narrow runway jutting out into the bay. One can almost look into people's bedroom windows as one lands. Within an hour of my arrival at the famous Mandarin Hotel a friend had collected me and driven me out to the new Sha Tin racecourse. Like the other racecourse, Happy Valley, almost in the centre of Hong Kong, it is administered by the Royal Hong Kong Jockey Club. Of the twelve stewards three or four are Chinese with names such as Li Fook Wo, Ping-Fan Fung, Hui Sai Fun. I was certainly transported very quickly into the atmosphere of this famous little island. Michael Tibbatts of Singapore was also Secretary of Sha Tin. The racing was nothing remarkable but I was fascinated by the vast crowd of gambling-mad Chinese. Such is their enthusiasm that when there is racing at Sha Tin thousands also go to Happy Valley, although there is no racing there, just to follow the racing on television, and bet. Equally fascinating was the sight of the Chinese with their noses glued to shop windows where they could observe the latest Stock-Exchange prices displayed there.

I thoroughly enjoyed my four scheduled days there; and no less my fifth, unscheduled day. As happens with many travellers I was caught out by the visa problem, so often experienced in visiting Australia. When I went down to the airport to book in on my flight to Brisbane the charming Chinese girl at the desk pointed out to me that my visa was invalid even though I had been to Australia within the last twelve months. A new visa is required for every visit, even if one goes to Australia six times in a single year. Kindly she booked me on to a flight next evening, promising to telex my friends, and told me where and how I could renew my visa. Knowing how long it takes in England to collect a visa I was somewhat apprehensive. Next morning, therefore, I went early to the Consulate, prepared to spend all day there. However, asked to produce evidence that I had been invited to Brisbane for a definite purpose I proffered a letter in which Eric Ixer had asked me if I could persuade Prince Philip, who was going to be at the Commonwealth Games, to visit the show 'as I know that you are a friend of his' – a statement at which I was duly flattered but, more important, one by which the authorities were duly impressed. Within an hour I had my visa. This not only enabled me to visit one of the best Chinese restaurants that I have ever been to in my life, but also, on leaving my hotel, to run straight into Mrs Thatcher who with her husband was lunching with the Governor, Sir Edward Youde, at the start of her negotiations on Hong Kong's future, as a result of which I followed the lengthy future negotiations with almost personal interest – which, of course, was quite ridiculous, but typical of human nature.

Brisbane

I arrived at Brisbane, twenty-four hours late, to be met by Anne Ixer and her and Eric's two delightful young daughters, Tina-Maria and Vera, who proved to be the most wonderful hosts. Having taken me to my hotel, The Zebra, they drove me out to Surfers' Paradise, the Gold Coast, where we had lunch, then to Andalucia Park where Eric showed me round the birds and animals and introduced me to the son of the proprietor, Mr Hans Van der Drift; his son turned out to be a pupil of Nuno d'Oliviera, the great Portuguese *haute-école*

maestro whom I had been responsible for bringing over to
England in 1966 to give a memorable display at the Horse of
the Year Show on his Andalucian stallions.

The following day we went to the Tambourine Mountains
and Binna Burna, the rain mountains. The scenery was
spectacular, with views right across to the Pacific Ocean. With
a cloudless sky it was like a perfect June day in England:
altogether a most enjoyable experience, with some lovely
amethyst to remind me of it.

Unfortunately the show, which started on the fourth day of
my visit, was very poorly attended. The hoped-for overflow
from the Commonwealth Games just did not materialise,
simply because the attendance at the Games was considerably
less than anticipated. Nor was the show helped by another big
show organised almost at the last minute in Canberra, to be
attended by the Queen and Prince Philip. In fact, the jumping,
with mostly local competitors, was of a high standard, with
two riders, Peter Mullins and David Williams (who have both
visited Europe) quite outstanding, the former riding a big grey
horse called Silverscreen which seemed to me as good a horse
as I had seen anywhere for a very long time – almost in the
Simona, Warwick Rex, Deister class. It never touched a fence
over Eric Ixer's excellent courses. I felt sorry for Eric and the
organisers at such disappointing support as they had worked
so hard. Nor was the situation helped from my point of view
by an appallingly bad loud-speaker system. It was after all the
main reason for my visit.

When on the way back to the hotel at the end of the show
Eric asked me what he owed me I felt really embarrassed. Yet
they were good enough to express the hope, quite sincerely,
that I would pay them another visit, which I assured them I
would very much like to, as I found Brisbane a pleasant,
spacious city, surrounded by beautiful countryside. In addition it had provided the legendary weather associated with
Australia, but which, thanks to my previous visits – when
there had been considerably more rain than sunshine – I had
begun to think it was a confidence trick or advertising gim-
mick. I was delighted at the end of 1984 to receive an invitation
to visit the new Pine Lodge Equestrian Centre at Thornlands,
Queensland, in the autumn of 1985.

On the way to the airport we stopped off to see State House, the old Governor's Residence. It is maintained as a museum, exactly as it might have been a hundred years ago. Full of atmosphere it gave one an idea of the lifestyle of those days. Beautiful lawns ran down to the river, where the Royal Yacht Britannia lay at anchor. I was sad to say goodbye to Queensland, the Ixers and their charming and friendly young daughters, but the parting was compensated a little when on boarding the plane the chief steward kindly promoted me to the almost empty first class – fillet steak *café de Paris*, Champagne sorbet! – which helped me on the twenty-eight hour flight to London and, within one and a half hours of landing, to the Horse of the Year Show at Wembley.

Chapter 12

Judge in a Cold Climate

I certainly do not share Jennifer's dislike of flying. As a rule I enjoy it, especially, needless to say, if one is fortunate enough to be travelling first class which, I always feel, is a holiday in itself. Nevertheless in principle I prefer not to travel by air in the winter months simply because, although it does not seem to happen too frequently, it is always possible that weather conditions will disrupt flights. Flying back from Portugal on one occasion in November our flight was diverted to Luton, which caused considerable problems. On another occasion flying to the Philippines my plane was the first to depart from London airport after a three-day hold-up because of snow. I have already described a flight from Paris in fog. I would never, however, be deterred from accepting an attractive invitation just because it meant flying in winter.

To judge home-bred stallions in Jutland in the winter of 1979 seemed a most intriguing assignment. So it was, but it entailed an appalling journey. We departed from Heathrow three hours late; we missed a connection in Copenhagen with the result that I had to stay overnight; and finally, after flying in terrifying conditions – non-stop snow storms – we were the last plane allowed to land at Kastrup, in a severe blizzard. I just do not know how we ever got down. I certainly was not surprised when once inside the airport I discovered that it was snowbound, so that it was impossible either to leave the airport or reach it. How the official from the show who was to meet me ever got through I shall never know. I can only say that the drive back to the show was both the most exciting I ever remember and an example of exceptionally brilliant driving. I arrived at the showground just ten minutes before my first class – hardly in a fit state to judge anything. But as so often is my experience the warmth of the hospitality soon made up for any inconvenience – and thawed me out.

Toronto

Certainly it never occurred to me not to accept an invitation to judge at the Royal Toronto Winter Fair just because it was in November. In fact, I had long harboured a secret hope that I might one day be invited; but I had always realised that it was a pious hope, as it was well known that only people with titles were ever invited from Britain to judge at the famous Winter Fair. By 1983, however, it seems that the show had run out of suitable titled people who had at least a smattering of knowledge about horses. Further, as Charles Baker, a member of the Show Executive Committee and a past President, later explained to me, when looking through the Hunters Improvement Society's panel of judges, from which the council were making their selection, he realised that there were only two names on the list that meant anything to him at all: Dick Francis and myself. So at last an aristocratic tradition was ended. Dick and I were the first fortunate commoners.

One was well aware, of course, that not much was expected of the invited English judge, as the American style of judging is so totally different to that in Britain. To begin with the horses are never ridden by the judges, who are not even expected to touch the horses. Everything is judged on style, which accords to a strict convention, basic conformation apparently being regarded as comparatively irrelevant. Nevertheless, fully aware that it was a great honour to be invited, making one the envy of every judge on the HIS panel, we accepted readily – Jennifer had been invited to accompany me – even though it meant missing the first fortnight of the hunting season.

On arriving at Heathrow we were agreeably surprised to be ushered immediately into the VIP lounge. On my return from Australia a few weeks earlier I had happened to mention to a friend, Rachel King, the excellent flights that I had had on BA to and from Brisbane. Her father is Lord King, Chairman of BA, whom I had known ever since as John King he was Master of the Belvoir and the owner of some good show horses and jumpers. I thought that he would probably appreciate a word of approval from a genuinely satisfied customer rather than the more usual complaint or criticism. As a result of this chance conversation some computer had detected the flight on which we were travelling and we found ourselves enjoying VIP treatment; we were finally almost the last to board the vast jumbo jet. On arrival at Toronto we were met by Rosemary Devlin, whom we had already met at the Royal Windsor Show, for many years a most popular hostess to foreign visitors at Toronto, and were taken in a large chauffeur-driven limousine to the Royal York Hotel where we were installed in a magnificent suite on the top floor. In each room there were bouquets of flowers and two huge baskets of fruit, one from the show and one from the hotel. In one basket there were mini-bottles of vodka and whisky, in the other cheese! Shortly after our arrival an even larger basket of fruit arrived, from Galen Weston. Who was he, we wondered? A little research reminded us that he was the son of Garfield Weston whose Fortnum and Mason empire he had inherited and who was, as we soon recalled, 'Prince Charles' polo-playing friend' who had narrowly escaped being kidnapped in Ireland. We had never met him before which made us appreciate the gift the more. He was, we discovered, a member of the Executive Committee.

I was soon enough in action, being summoned, despite any possible jet lag, to a 7.30 a.m. breakfast in the suite of the Chairman, a charming friendly person, Moffat Dunlap, and Diana, his new young wife with whom Jennifer was to become very friendly. My co-judges, Pam Arthur and Michael Page, were also present. Pam lived in Columbia where she was a well known instructor and a joint-Master of the Fraser Valley Hunt; she had emigrated from Sussex twenty years earlier. Michael Page came from his home in New York which he used as a base for his many judging and 'clinic' commitments. He had been a member of the American Three-Day Event Team from 1959 to 1968, winning the individual bronze medal in the Mexico Olympics. Both seemed congenial and realistically helpful. I had little doubt that I would get on well with them though, as I made clear from the start, I would be little more than a cipher as far as the judging was concerned.

We were driven down to the Coliseum, a complex similar to Earl's Court or Olympia, though possibly larger, to commence judging the junior classes at 9.00 a.m. The first class, for hunter ponies, had some twenty entries, but only half an hour was allowed for judging, which was ten minutes more than for most classes. To begin with I felt a complete passenger, but Pam and Michael were most expeditious, seemingly agreeing on each entry. 'Style' is everything. If, for instance, a horse 'misses' – that is 'puts in a short one' – it is virtually eliminated. If a horse jumps even slightly to the right or left it is harshly marked down. If it hits one of the eight simple fences it is out: not actually eliminated, but marked so low that it could not possibly be placed. In other words, it is detail that is all-important, rather than the general impression, other than overall smoothness which counts very high. The result is that often a comparatively dull, plain and uninspiring horse wins at the expense of the sort of horse that most even moderately experienced horsemen would prefer to own. Conformation scarcely comes into it; most judges in any event ignore the percentage of marks that conformation is supposed to carry. After the jumping is completed each horse not eliminated is just trotted up to the centre of the ring from the collecting ring, principally to show that it is sound; but that is the only oportunity that a judge has to consider conformation, other than in the actual conformation classes. These are usually judged in the collecting ring; the horses are led in at the walk, run up at the trot, lined up, and the judge then sorts them into the final order. The judging is all done at breathtaking pace which is probably easy enough with very experienced judges, but bewildering to a beginner. The experts can tell at a glance if a horse measures up, either in style or in conformation; though one could not help feeling that there is a certain amount of judging on 'form': but where is there not?

It was certainly a most interesting experience and, by the end of the show I did begin to feel that I was getting the hang of it, thinking on the same lines as my co-judges. I even had sufficient confidence to insist, on the last day of the show, that a rosette, albeit a lowly one, was awarded to the only horse that I should like to have taken home: a real substancy middleweight chestnut with a grand outlook and tremendous power behind the saddle.

In all I judged some twenty classes, apart from numerous championships, spread over ten days. Obviously this became a little repetitive, even tedious, as so many of the same horses appeared in different classes. It also left much time when one was unoccupied as one might have a class at 9.00 a.m., then not another until 1.30 p.m. with no further commitment until the beginning of the evening session at 7.00 p.m. Naturally one hesitated to ask for a car to take one back to the hotel too often. Indeed, there was much of interest besides the show classes to watch at the show – some sections, indeed, that we found as interesting, or even more interesting, than the show classes. There was some first-class jumping over Alan Oliver's excellent courses with, surprisingly, the newly motivated Swiss tending to dominate. We particularly liked the iron-grey Percherons – really superb horses – and the Belgians, a Canadian Breed of heavy horses with which we were not previously familiar. We spent many hours in the morning watching these being judged, in a manner with which we were far more familiar. We really enjoyed, too, the Roadsters which go faster and faster and faster, not infrequently tipping over. These had the audience on their feet at every performance. There were also some fine coaches and fours judged by Major Chamberlain Macdonald from Hampshire, as well as the Mounties on the big nights attended by the Minister of Agriculture or the Governor General.

At every evening performance one had to wear full evening dress, including top hat! If one was a hunting person one had to wear a red evening coat. Possessing, now, only one starched shirt this presented something of a problem, hotel laundry service in Canada not, seemingly, being very familiar with starched shirts. Jennifer had to wear a full-length evening dress each night, which could well have been awkward for her also, had not friends rallied round. When 'off duty' one was allotted seats in one of the 'boxes' – blocks of seats railed off with coloured rope – that were all round the arena at the front of the stands. One evening Michael Page was refused admission to one of the boxes as he was only in a dinner jacket and had no hat!

There were, of course, plenty of social activities. The first evening we were invited to a splendid reception and dinner by the President, Colonel Allan Barton, to whom I took a great liking. Next day there was a Canada Equestrian Federation reception at the Holiday Inn where I met again Jean Driver, representing the Federation from Calgary. After the reception we visited the famous tower with its revolving restaurant at the top, giving wonderful views of the city, with Philip Drew, the Chairman of the British Show Jumping Association, who was a show-jumping judge at the Winter Fair, and his wife, with both of whom we became very friendly. One afternoon we were invited to the racing at Greenwood by Charles Baker, Chairman of the Ontario Jockey Club. We were entertained in the Trustees' Suite which on a bitterly cold day enabled us to watch all the racing from behind glass, and an excellent lunch was served after the second of the nine races. My co-judges kindly took us out to dinner one evening at a very good 'down town' restaurant, Geo Bigliardi. We were also fortunate to meet Jill Hermant, who had been a bridesmaid at my niece Patricia's wedding and was now married to a Canadian, living in Toronto. We spent a very pleasant evening with them at their home in one of the 'superior' suburbs. One evening we had an amusing chop-stick dinner before the show at a well known Japanese restaurant with John and Rosemary Devlin. I could not help feeling that it must have been the first time that anyone had ever eaten at a Japanese restaurant in full hunt evening dress, red coat, top hat, the lot! We were also taken to a smart Italian restaurant, Il Posto, by Dan Owen who, as a Canadian friend of Bill and Toren Fieldhouse, near neighbours of ours at Buckingham, often comes over for a day's hunting with the Whaddon Chase.

But the highlight of our entertainment, perhaps, was the visit to a meet of the Toronto and North York Hunt at Harold Crang's country home. We enjoyed being driven sixty miles out into the country, right away from the not very inspiring city of Toronto; it was, also, a pleasure to have the opportunity of spending time with Harold Crang, so often a visitor to the Horse of the Year Show at Wembley, and for many years probably the most influential personality at the Toronto Winter Fair of which he had been President in the late fifties.

He had a most attractive house, surrounded by glorious scenery, particularly impressive in the 'fall', despite the bitter cold. There was a field of about sixty, most of the men in scarlet, all wearing proper crash helmets with harness. There it is, apparently, completely taken for granted. I was sorry not to have been able to accept the invitation of a mount, but I was committed to the official show lunch back in the city. After a lavish stirrup-cup hounds moved off at about 10.15 a.m. Harold Crang took us in his car to watch them draw a long plantation. Pointing to a small covert in the valley Harold told me that it was there that they had killed their last fox. On enquiring how long ago that was, expecting that it would have been a week or two previously, I was informed that it was four years ago!

Apparently they do not really expect to catch foxes, there not being all that many, nor indeed specifically to hunt a fox; anything will do. The main purpose is to 'ride to hounds', jumping a few fences; those who want to, that is. There is an official 'Hill-toppers' group with an appointed leader who guides his party to vantage points where they can see the fun without jumping anything. When I had to leave for the lunch with Harold Crang and a friend of his, John Higgins, who turned out to be David Westmorland's brother-in-law, Jennifer stayed on with others in the party, continuing to follow the hunt, though she did not see much sport as they never found, or so it seemed to her. At the stroke of twelve o'clock hunting was called off, and the whole field repaired to the hunt 'breakfast', for which the men exchanged red coats for their hunt blazers. When asked if this was a regular custom Jennifer was told that it was all part of the day's hunting, 'just like England'. It seemed politic not to divulge that hunt breakfasts had not, except on very special occasions, been held in England for 100 years.

Meanwhile, back at the Royal York I discovered that I had had the honour to be one of the ten or twelve invited to a special reception to meet the Governor General. He was an amiable, slightly ill-at-ease person, previously, I learned, a Socialist Member of Parliament who had suddenly been selected by Trudeau to replace the intended new Governor General – an elder statesman of politics – after he had already arrived in London to be officially appointed by the Queen. When introduced we both seemed somewhat lost for words until looking closely at my tie he asked me what could possibly be the club that it represented. I explained that it was my Whaddon Chase Hunt Supporters Club tie, which elicited no comment from him. Stiffly he passed on without comment to the person standing next to me. However, when I found myself being privileged to sit at the top table at this vast lunch – for 600 – we got on very much better. He seemed generally interested in my background and my opinion of the show, while I found him human and modest – and honest. He admitted that he had never before been to the Toronto Winter Fair: 'It is not really in my line.'

At the end of the show there was a reception at the Coliseum at which there were presentations for which I had not been prepared. Even less was I prepared to be called up first, as a judge from Britain, realising to my horror as Moffat Dunlap pushed the microphone towards me that I was expected to say a few words. Seeing my dismay Moffat whispered: 'Just tell them the story that you told me earlier', which I did. As I had hurried out of the Royal York Hotel, all dolled up in full evening dress, red coat, top hat, to the great chauffeur-driven limousine waiting to take me to the show, a scruffy-looking man in dirty jeans and an anorak approached me and asked me to hail him a taxi, obviously taking me for the commission-aire. It brought the house down; but perhaps there was a significant hint in this anecdote. Is this famous show living a little too much in the past? Is there room now for modernisa-tion? In similar vain one wonders whether the show is still justified in inviting a judge all the way from England – titled or untitled – at great expense, almost as a prestige gesture, when it is virtually impossible for the English judge to contribute anything really worthwhile at all, other than on the social side, the techniques of judging in Britain and North America being so totally different. Enormously as we had enjoyed our stay in Toronto, the privilege of being a part of the famous Toronto Winter Fair, and all the generous hospitality, yet we almost felt guilty; we had contributed so little and it had cost the show so much. Jennifer, being a realist, and a regular show exhibitor herself, suggested that were it not for the cost of inviting us from England the prizes for the show classes – on average about £60 for the winner – might have been increased. Travel costs and accommodation at the Royal York must be astronomic. Nevertheless it cannot be denied that we were sad to say goodbye to the many friends that we had made in Toronto, especially the Devlins and Dunlaps – whose baby we were delighted to hear arrived safely a few weeks later. Who were we to question the show's generosity? Indeed we were, surely, the last people to question the show's policy of inviting 'distinguished' judges from overseas. It was just that we felt that our contribution had been so minimal.

Waiting with Alan Oliver in the departure lounge I was surprised to be called to the information desk where, it was announced, the British Airways Manager wished to see me. I made my way to the desk and stood there waiting, wondering what it could all be about. On a previous occasion we had discovered that Jennifer's passport was out of date. I also recalled my lack of visa at Hong Kong a few weeks earlier. After a few minutes the extremely impressive manager, in the livery of British Airways, arrived.

'May I see your boarding passes?'

I handed them to him, confidently: he looked at them – then, to my horror tore them up.

'I am exchanging them for these', he said, handing two first-class boarding passes. 'Compliments of the management. Have a good flight.'

We certainly did: *saumon fumé d'Ecosse à la russe, sole waleska, pâté chaude de giber, contrefilet de boeuf rôti a l'Anglaise; tarte aux pêches meringue.* Some people are lucky. We were more than ever pleased to have been invited, though we experienced a tinge of guilt leaving Alan Oliver in the tourist class; but at Heathrow he assured us that we need not have worried. Having built over thirty different courses he had slept soundly all the way. Conscious of my own humble stint I should, perhaps, have felt guilty again. But as we enjoyed our *sole waleska*, washed down with champagne, I cannot remember any such feeling.

It had been yet another wonderful trip thanks to our hosts and the organisers.

Epilogue

Signing Off – Almost Literally!

The foregoing chapters will have shown that almost without exception my professional travels have been enjoyable. The experience of landing in the fog at Geneva was not pleasant, but I can honestly say that I was not for one moment seriously or consciously frightened. Perhaps it all happened too quickly. Nor was landing in a blizzard at Karstrup much to enjoy, but I knew that air liners did land in blizzards; indeed, I knew that permission would be given to land only if conditions were possible. I remembered, too, that pilots were just as keen to get safely home as their passengers. My emotion at Karstrup was rather one of annoyance. How, in such conditions, would I be able to get to the show on time?

My final anecdote, however, is a very different story. I really was very frightened; indeed, I even resigned myself to the fact that this must be the end. It all added to my store of experiences, but was one that I would happily have foregone.

It was 1968. At rather short notice the BBC had asked me to fly to Brussels to cover an international event on the Friday evening of their show. I was not very happy about this as, in the first place, it was the night of our Hunt Ball which was being held at Pendley. Apart from the fact that we had, of course, arranged a big dinner-party, I felt that both in my position as Master of the Hunt and as the owner of Pendley I should be there in the role of host. Secondly, I realised that it would mean my missing hunting on the Saturday. I reminded the BBC of the clause in my contract whereby I did not have to do a programme on a Saturday between 1 November and 31 March. It was pointed out that the programme was on a Friday, recorded, in fact, for transmission in 'Grandstand' the following afternoon.

Although for some reason that I cannot remember it was the first competition of the evening that was being recorded, I realised that it would never be finished in time for me to catch the last plane out of Brussels. I then recalled that I had a friend who, at that time, regularly took part in the Shakespeare Festival at Pendley and as I remembered was connected with civil flying. I contacted him to find out whether it would be possible to hire a light aircraft – with pilot, of course – to fly me to Brussels and back that evening. He assured me that there would be no problem, and that he could lay it all on for me. He also told me what it would cost.

I phoned the BBC to see if they would be prepared to pay for it. They would not but, generously, appreciating my plight, if not understanding it, they agreed to pay for me for a first-class flight. This, together, with the one night's subsistence to which I was entitled came to little more than hiring the private plane. Accordingly I went ahead with the plan, confident that I could be back at Pendley by 11.00 p.m., which in any event was as early as most people were likely to arrive at the Ball.

I suggested to David Satow that he might like to join me. He would, I was sure, enjoy it and it would be company for me. David was then living in a cottage of ours at Foscote. We had just accomplished the great move of the British Horse Society and the British Show Jumping Association from Bedford Square, London, to Stoneleigh where David had switched from his position with the BSJA to the British Horse Society as Development Officer. He was delighted to accept my invitation, and so, at three o'clock in the afternoon of 12 November, we set off for Luton airport. We soon contacted our pilot, who turned out to be a charming German, cleared customs and boarded our plane. It was a ridiculous feeling as we became airborne within less than 100 yards of our launch down the two-mile runway, but the flight on a bright, blustery autumn afternoon was pure joy as we hedge-hopped across the Eastern Counties, skimmed over the variety of vessels in the Channel and threaded our way through the suburbs into Schipol airport.

Parking the aircraft 'somewhere round the back' our pilot escorted us to the relevant authorities and arranged where we

should meet him on our return from the show at about
9.30 p.m. We then took a taxi to the stadium where we
received a warm welcome, and were wined and dined by the
Eurovision producer. (It had been considered unnecessary for
me to have a BBC liaison on this little trip.) Not surprisingly
the show started more than half an hour late, which did not
matter, of course, as it was being recorded, though I did
remark to David that it was fortunate that it was not the last
competition that we were covering as it was doubtful if that
would finish before 2.00 a.m.– not unusual in continental
shows. In fact, it was 9.30 p.m. before we left the showground, by the time that all the formalities had been completed. We then could not find a taxi. No taxis were arriving,
as the show had commenced two hours earlier and no taxis
were yet coming to pick up customers at the end of the show,
at least two hours hence.

It had turned very cold, which meant a long drafty wait
before at about 10.15 p.m. a taxi turned up. We asked the
driver to take us to the airport as quickly as possible, which he
did; but when we arrived there was no sign of our pilot at the
appointed place. Eventually we traced him to the office of the
flight manager – or some such. He looked embarrassed to see
us.

'Anything wrong?' I asked.

'Bad news', he replied.

'What?'

Initially attempting to suggest that it was our fault because
we were an hour late, he informed us that we could not reach
Luton before their customs closed; we would not be allowed
to land without customs clearance. In fact, he had just forgotten to check the Luton customs which, it transpired, closed
automatically at 10.00 p.m.

Where else could we land, then?

Nowhere.

Blackbush, I suggested.

Also closed.

Then we would have to fly to London. Out of the question!
He seemed horrified. Gatwick? Quite impossible. Only very
exceptionally are light aircraft allowed to land at major ter-
minals. Virtually never from overseas.

So what? There was nothing for it apparently but to doss down in the airport lounge for the night and take off at 5.00 a.m., reaching Luton in time for customs clearance at about 6.30 a.m. To say that I was furious is an understatement. All the planning, the cost, the inconvenience all round – but there was nothing for it. I managed to phone Jennifer at Pendley, and resigned myself to the thought of the Ball carrying on quite happily without me!

By the time that we had returned to the departure lounge it was almost deserted; the last flight out had departed at about 11.00 p.m. The bar's grill had just been brought down; the coffee counter was closed. We found a couple of shiny green leather benches and dossed down, using our brief-cases as pillows. It did not seem as though we had fitfully dozed for more than a few minutes when we were awakened by an insistent whirring, accompanied by occasional splashing and swilling. Sure enough, it was 3.00 a.m. and the cleaners had arrived. As they swept and swilled around our benches we were lucky not to get soaked. Further sleep was impossible so we just rose and wandered around until it was nearly 5.00 a.m. Our pilot appeared – goodness knows from where – to inform us that he was going to prepare the aircraft: would we join him there? We told him that we had as little chance of finding his aircraft as we would of finding the North Pole; we must accompany him – fortunately, as it was only with the greatest difficulty that he found the aircraft himself.

By about 5.30 a.m. we were aboard and taxi-ing out for take-off. It was only just light, but though rather raw, it was not an unpleasant morning; quite good for hunting, I thought, having estimated that I should have no trouble in getting to the meet in time as it was only about six miles from Foscote. Had I known what we were to experience before reaching home there is little doubt that I would have returned to the airport and awaited the first official Sabena flight. But, of course, there was no way that I could have known: or was there? I am no authority on aeronautics.

It was still quite dark when we took off, and misty, but we were soon airborne and flying happily over the sleepy suburbs at about 3,000 feet. As we flew out over the coast it was obvious from the choppy seas below that the weather was fairly rough. As we crossed the Channel we climbed another 1,000 feet or so. Our pilot was in constant chat over the intercom. Once he appeared to try to call up Luton, but apparently it was not yet operative.

Rather as when approaching Geneva in the fog I had not at first appreciated that what I took to be streaks of rain down the window were young saplings, so now I did not at first appreciate just what we were flying into. In the dim light of dawn it all seemed to merge into the sea and the murky weather through which we were flying. Suddenly I realised that it was a dense wall of cloud that stretched from the sea to the sky. As we approached this wall it loomed nearer and nearer almost like the massive Chair fence must look to jockeys as they see it stretching across the course in front of them at Aintree. I looked round at David Satow sitting behind me. He made a grimace. Having been dropped behind the lines in Yugoslavia with Fitzroy Maclean he was probably more used to unorthodox aircraft and less than straight-forward flights than I was.

Suddenly we hit this massive wall of turbulence; and indeed it was almost like hitting something solid. The plane shuddered and bounced, swerving this way and that, seemingly almost out of control. I would not have been surprised had the plane nose-dived into a spin. Doubtless it was only the skill of the pilot that prevented it. I hoped that perhaps this bank of cloud was just a mile or so in depth and that we would soon be through it. Far from it. In fact, as we learned later, it stretched from the east coast of England to the south-west. The plane within seconds had become the proverbial shuttlecock, tossed hither and thither in the appalling, relentless weather. Visibility extended to the wing tips and the propellers, no further. Nor did we seem to be achieving any forward progress. The pilot was increasingly busy on the intercom, though because of the interference it was not possible for me to hear what was being said to him. I could only judge from his tone and his expression that he was receiving very little of what might be termed helpful information.

After five or ten nerve-wracking minutes there was suddenly a break in the cloud. For a few moments one could actually see the ground and in those minutes there, easily discernible, was, miraculously, an air strip. Presumably it was Lymn. In a few seconds it had gone, but to me it seemed to provide a solution to our problems. Clutching the pilot's arm I pointed downwards: 'Lymn', I shouted, 'just below!'

He nodded.

'Why can't we drop through this cloud and land there?'

He turned and looked at me, incredulous.

'Land there? I'd lose my licence.'

'Why on earth?'

'No customs clearance.'

'But surely –' I turned to David for support, but disappointingly he just shook his head.

After a few minutes of desperate buffeting through the swirling cloud I clutched the pilot's arm again: 'Frankly I'd rather you lost your licence than I lost my life', I yelled.

He said nothing, just battled on. Then I remembered Manston. I had been at school in Thanet, only a few miles from Lymn, and had been associated with that part of the world ever since. Manston aerodrome. RAF at one time, I thought. Now? – it did not matter.

'Manston', I yelled. 'Manston aerodrome, near Margate.'

After a moment's thought he picked up a book from a shelf, looked through it, presumably for a code. Within a couple of minutes we were in touch with Manston I could hear him asking permission to land. I could not hear the reply, but with a shrug of the shoulders he put down his book and told me gruffly, that it was not possible; only one runway, hurricane-force cross wind; not safe. Was it not worth risking? I asked. Again he shrugged his shoulders, but after several more minutes he made contact with Manston again. They were adamant: we could not attempt a landing – far too dangerous.

Where else? I thought desperately. Biggin Hill, Croydon, Gatwick? – of course, Gatwick. That must be the answer – in a crisis like this. Whatever bureaucratic objections there might be.

'What about Gatwick?' He gave a hollow, mocking laugh, but after a few more minutes when it seemed inevitable that our plane must very soon break up he managed to make contact with Luton. I sensed that he was asking advice. Obviously we had insufficient petrol to reach Luton, so the situation really was now desperate. Oddly enough it was not entirely fear that possessed me as much annoyance with myself. Why on earth had I been so foolish – so vain, arrogant? – to feel that I had to get back for the Hunt Ball and the hunting next day, organising this ridiculous trip – in the middle of winter? I glanced back at David, but he was just sitting there very grim, looking rather grey. He seemed indisposed to talk. Rather limply I just said 'Sorry, David', and tried to smile, a sort of smile of resignation! There was no point in panicking. Anyway we were entirely in the hands of our pilot.

Suddenly I realised that the pilot had made contact with Gatwick, but it was clear that they were being totally unsympathetic. Eventually, it seemed, they suggested that he should contact Heathrow. Their refusal there to help appeared to be very brief and to the point; indeed, their attitude seemed to be that they could not be bothered with small fry if they were stupid enough to get themselves into difficulties. Our pilot shrugged again; his face was covered with perspiration.

'What about Northolt?' I shouted desperately. He ignored me. The weather, if that were possible, seemed to have deteriorated. It was a miracle to me that our poor little plane was still airborne. As though in utter despair our pilot contacted Gatwick once again. His voice was quite different. No longer cold, professional, it was appealing, almost desperate: a May Day voice, surely.

'OK', I heard him say, at the same time turning and giving me a thumbs-up sign. Relief spread all over his face – and mine.

'How do we find it?'

With some difficulty, it now being so indistinct, I was able to make out Gatwick's unbelievable reply.

'Drop down to 1,500 ft. Find the coast, turn west. Fly along the coast until you reach Brighton. When you see the first pier turn right, follow the London road until you reach Peas Blossom where you will see the lights over the roundabout at the head of the motorway which bears right. Bear left and as soon as you are over the Crawley ridge you will see our lights. We'll talk you down.'

We followed the instructions to the letter. At the top of the M23 we bore left. Below the cloud level it was, of course, very

much smoother though weather conditions were still
unpleasant. We could see the rising ground ahead. At least I
could; but could our pilot? Exhausted? Disorientated? Asleep
even? I just do not know, but I was suddenly aware that we
were flying straight into the ridge. I grabbed him by the arm.
'Higher, surely, higher!' I urged. Immediately he pulled back
the stick – and we cleared the summit with what seemed like
only a few feet to spare!

The moment that we were on the other side they started
talking us down. Fasten your seat belts! Were we really going
to make it? I watched anxiously as the Gatwick lights
approached. Lower, lower, lower. Bump! bump! We were
down within a few feet of the southernmost part of the
runway. As the plane taxied a hundred yards down the
runway, slowing all the time, suddenly over the intercom
there was a deafening shout, terrifying in its authority and
anger. 'For Christ's sake get off the runway, you – !' We
veered sharply to the left on to the grass. As we did so a huge
Sabena airliner landed behind us, almost bouncing over the
top of us. The first passenger flight out of Brussels!

We all sat for several minutes without moving. Eventually
the pilot restarted the engine and brought the plane nearer the
building, as he did so pointing to the petrol gauge – with
another shrug. Presumably it was empty. I cannot remember
looking. We climbed out and set off on legs of jelly to the
airport building. Halfway across, coming up behind David
called out, 'Don't you want your brief-case?' I hardly cared.
The person in charge of whatever office it was to which we
were taken gave us some coffee. It was just 7.25 a.m.

We declined the offer of our pilot to fly us on later in the
morning to Luton. We preferred the train to Victoria, tube to
St Pancras and the train again to Luton. Our taxi from the
station reached the airport at 10.00 a.m.

'What about hunting?' David asked. 'I don't think so.
Anyway, it's too late. Just let's go to the meet at Warren Farm,
where I know Mr Turney will have plenty of the hard stuff on
the sideboard; and that, I think, is what is needed.'

It was my intention to come out with the second horses at
about two o'clock: but when I got home at midday I fell asleep
straight away, not waking until four o'clock. Realistically

Jennifer had decided that it was senseless to wake me up.

A strange pendant to this tale. That evening David Satow came up for a drink. At 9.00 p.m. we turned on the news. Earlier in the evening an airliner had crashed into Crawley ridge on its approach to Gatwick. There were no survivors.

This final chapter was written in a little corner of paradise in Barbados where we were staying with Carol Parsons, a pony-breeding friend of Jennifer's and her husband, Peter. But even all the exotic beauty of the Caribbean could not erase each hair-raising detail of the flight from Brussels to Gatwick that November morning in 1968; certainly the least enjoyable experience in the travels of this commentator. But in truth it was the only unpleasant one, which cannot be a bad record over thirty years.

Index